D1106304

THE MAKING OF A DANCER

Also by Arnold L. Haskell

THE SCULPTOR SPEAKS (*Heinemann*)

★

BALLETOMANIA (*Gollancz*)
DIAGHILEFF (*Gollancz*)
DANCING ROUND THE WORLD (*Gollancz*)
BALLET PANORAMA (*Batsford*)
FELICITY DANCES (*Nelson*)
PRELUDE TO BALLET (*Nelson*)
BALLET (*Pelican*)
BALLETOMANE'S SCRAPBOOK (*A. & C. Black*)
BALLETOMANE'S ALBUM (*A. & C. Black*)
BALLET—TO POLAND (*A. & C. Black*)
THE NATIONAL BALLET (*A. & C. Black*)

★

WALTZING MATILDA (*A. & C. Black*)
AUSTRALIA (*Collins*)
THE AUSTRALIANS (*A. & C. Black*)

Australia and New Zealand
THE OXFORD UNIVERSITY PRESS, MELBOURNE
Canada
THE MACMILLAN COMPANY OF CANADA, TORONTO
South Africa
THE OXFORD UNIVERSITY PRESS, CAPE TOWN
India and Burma
MACMILLAN AND COMPANY LIMITED
BOMBAY CALCUTTA MADRAS

From a drawing by
EDWARD ROBERTSON

THE MAKING OF A DANCER

and other Papers on the
Background to Ballet

by

ARNOLD L. HASKELL

WITH TWELVE PHOTOGRAPHS
AND A FRONTISPIECE

ADAM & CHARLES BLACK
4, 5 & 6 SOHO SQUARE LONDON W.1
1946

FIRST PUBLISHED 1946

MADE IN GREAT BRITAIN
PRINTED BY MORRISON AND GIBB LTD., LONDON AND EDINBURGH

CONTENTS

ILLUSTRATIONS

MANIFESTO BY WAY OF INTRODUCTION

Dedicated to

MADAME ADELINE GENÉE

PRESIDENT OF THE ROYAL ACADEMY OF DANCING

for her patience and her constant sense of humour in and out of the Chair and, as she would wish, to my fellow-members of her Committee on the understanding that neither she nor they are in any way committed to agree either with my views or my expression of them.

MANIFESTO BY WAY OF INTRODUCTION

i. *The Lectures and the Audience*

THESE lectures were given under the auspices of the Royal Academy of Dancing who sponsored a tour starting in Edinburgh and Glasgow and finishing in Exeter. Some of them I had given previously both for C.E.M.A. and the Regional Committee for the Education of H.M. Forces in various parts of Great Britain : well over 1000 lectures in all.

The major part of the text published here was taken down in shorthand during the lectures and I have made the bare minimum of alterations, merely removing those jokes to which the medium of print was unkind, various local references and some repetition of matter that is necessarily common to several of the lectures. As it is, many general ideas have been repeated, a good thing judging from the advice given me by a famous headmaster : " Repeat everything seven times when speaking to children, ten times to adults." I have omitted three historical lectures as the subject-matter can be found elsewhere.

My audiences were of the most diverse : army, navy and air force, miners, factory workers, education authorities, school-children, boys and girls in Grammar and Public schools, music, arts and ballet clubs, Rotarians and Soroptimists, dancing teachers and their pupils. Of all these the outstanding audiences have been in the Forces and in schools of general education. They have never failed to ask many and searching questions ; in the Army Education centres over an hour of questioning is invariable. In the schools I have always met with extraordinary co-operation from the staff. No lecturer on whatever subject —and I have lectured on very different subjects in schools— could wish for a more alert and stimulating audience than a group of girls round school certificate age. They are critical and interested and prevent a lecturer from adopting some easy formula that has proved successful with the less alert grown-ups. The contrast between these girls and their older sisters in the youth clubs is astonishing. It speaks for the need not only of an extended period of schooling but of Arts Centres of the type that C.E.M.A.[1] advocates. In those centres where the influence of C.E.M.A. has been active over a long period the difference in the reaction of the audience is most noticeable. In Mansfield, Notts, for instance, I have given seven lectures on ballet to large and interested audiences, yet no ballet company has visited Mansfield. The audiences have been built up by the librarian and curator, Mr. Cronshaw ; C.E.M.A. and the M.O.I. have provided him with musicians, exhibitions and speakers. His art gallery has become a real centre of education. Equally striking has been the case of the Forces Centre at Salisbury where Warrant Officer John Coulson, B.E.M., has created a model centre of Adult Education making an exhibition or a concert into a real event. Such collaboration between C.E.M.A., a local man with drive and purpose and the scholastic authorities will play a major role in creating critical audiences for the arts. Many a grim-looking industrial centre has given me a pleasurable shock through the numbers and the quality of its audience. I mention numbers, but we must be careful not to be taken in by statistics. Often a group of from twenty-five to fifty gives better and more lasting results than an audience of hundreds.

But of all my audiences the most disappointing have been the members of the dancing profession. When they do turn up they sit completely dumb at question time, although every word of the lecture is of immediate concern to them. " Can you wonder at it ? " said an enlightened teacher to me. " They have all left school far too early to understand what it is all about. Now if you were lecturing on how to turn a *pirouette*, you would have had a queue from here to the Midland Hotel."

[1] Now the Arts Council of Great Britain. I have an affection for the old name.

ii. *The Profession and the Royal Academy of Dancing*

Some time ago my friend, P. J. S. Richardson, editor of *The Dancing Times*, and co-founder with me of the Camargo Society, said to me, " None of you writers give sufficient credit to the rank and file of the dancing teachers for the present state of our ballet." He was, of course, perfectly correct, if by rank and file, he meant some fifteen hard-working, intelligent and really selfless teachers who are an honour to the profession. The general public, and even the large and devoted ballet public, knows nothing of the vast teaching profession or of what takes place in the classroom. That is the case in every art ; outside the profession the teacher gets very little credit. In one particular, however, ballet is quite exceptional ; the teacher-pupil relationship often persists throughout a career and even the greatest ballerina looks to her teacher to correct faults of technique, and to give her continual refresher courses. One of the first questions a professional asks is, " Who was So-and-so's teacher ? " The teaching of ballet is—or should be—an aristocratic art in the sense that one can trace the pedigree from pupil to teacher right back to the very origins of ballet.

There are two types of teacher ; one who has been a great executant, such as Preobrajenska, Egorova, Kchesinska, Legat, Cecchetti, Karsavina and others, and the teacher who has never been on the stage and who sets out from the very first to work up a connection. It is with the second group that we are now concerned. Their reputation, often deservedly very considerable, is confined to the dancing profession.

Now there is nothing to prevent anyone without the slightest qualification setting up as a teacher of dancing, and doing untold harm as a result. Were I to name any such teaching quacks the result would be a libel suit which I should most certainly lose—they are protected far more completely than their unfortunate pupils. There are safeguards, but the ordinary parent may very easily be in complete ignorance of them and it is worth while giving the matter the widest publicity.

The Association of Operatic Dancing was formed in 1920 with Adeline Genée as president and Philip Richardson, whose work for dancing in all its branches has been tremendous, as secretary-treasurer. It has an exceptionally strong committee consisting of leaders of the art and the profession of dancing, as well as people of experience in other walks of life, all of whom give up a great deal of their time in its interests. Its original title always seemed to me singularly ill-chosen as it linked ballet with opera, and in that partnership ballet has always been a very junior and barely tolerated partner. Such a relationship, in fact, was not contemplated by the new association. Its aim was the vital one of laying down a definite standard of teaching to be attained and maintained by a series of examinations. No teacher, with the exception of certain great artists clearly qualified by experience, was recognised by the Association unless qualified by examination. The serious teacher immediately realised that membership of the Association was the best way of safeguarding her interests.[1] In this way many parents began to understand that the examinations would help their daughters, not only from a stage point of view but more especially in taking up teaching as a profession. The Association's influence grew to such an extent that in 1935 it received official recognition in the form of a royal charter, becoming the Royal Academy of Dancing. As such, it was the youngest Academy of Dancing in the world, and dancing was the last of the muses to be so honoured in this country. At last it had rid itself of the frivolous association of the naughty 'nineties and had gained a patent of respectability long overdue.

Now there is a sharp distinction between our Royal Academy of Dancing and those famous state Academies in France, Russia

[1] It must be made quite clear that the Academy has always been refreshingly free from any mumbo-jumbo. It recognises the great individual teacher and artist who does not happen to be a member and has often invited a distinguished non-member to join a panel of judges. We are discussing the average case here.—A. L. H.

and Denmark. This distinction is all-important. Our Academy represents a typical British compromise. It respects the individuality of the private teacher so long as she conforms to a certain minimum standard, and as a member of the family it gives her not only protection but numerous advantages. In fact she receives more advantages from her membership of the Academy than the Academy at the moment receives from her. " Think of the teachers " is the worthy but somewhat stultifying cry that inevitably arises when some worthwhile reform is mooted. It is noteworthy that those teachers closely associated with the Academy's work fully realise the position and are only guided by the thought of the welfare of their art. This Academy is very much more than an association of teachers. It is a policy-forming body. Its position is therefore a difficult one that requires constantly tactful guidance. It may have very definite ideas on a number of subjects and many very clear aims in view, but at times it hesitates to legislate rapidly since many of those aims might seriously disrupt the individual teacher's livelihood or, what is more common, might appear at first sight to do so. It must continually educate and guide. Viewed in this, the only practical manner, it has achieved much during its short career. It has given a vast number of extreme individualists a true feeling of *esprit-de-corps* and has begun to raise the entire standard of teaching in this country ; a move that must be greatly accelerated.

iii. *Miss Hopjump and Miss Somerville, M.A.*

I must make it quite clear at this point that the survey of teaching that follows, the criticism and the suggested programme are entirely personal, though I have every reason to know that they meet with the approval of the majority who feel these subjects deeply.

Let us take the case of little Miss Hopjump who teaches

dancing in a large Midlands town. She knows her technique well enough to be an advanced member of the Royal Academy, but ballet is not her mainstay since the majority of her pupils demand tap and acrobatic. Her education has stopped short of school certificate and the only ballet she has seen is an occasional performance of the Sadler's Wells or International Ballets. Indeed she has never really thought of ballet as an art. It is a part of her livelihood and if her pupils get through their exams and win an occasional competition, she is very well satisfied.

Miss Somerville, M.A., is headmistress of the Girls' High School in the same town. She is interested in many outside activities and eager to get the best for her girls in artistic education. She takes great pride in her music and art departments. Miss Hopjump and Miss Somerville never meet, though the dancing teacher's name is at times a source of irritation to the headmistress when girls ask for time off to attend some dancing function. The school's dancing is dealt with by the gym mistress.

Poor Miss Hopjump is in a totally false position. She is teaching an art without any knowledge of what it is all about. She cannot convince the headmistress that the dance should be a part of school education and even were Miss Somerville already convinced she would certainly never call upon Miss Hopjump for her services. Probably this does not worry Miss Hopjump in the slightest. She is doing very well already and has no need of the extra work. The trouble is that it is damaging ballet, the school's dancing, and doing no good to the Academy whose initials she is entitled to print after her name.

The Hopjumps—and they are legion—are the greatest problem in the dancing profession to-day. One can no longer say that they are unqualified to teach steps, their examination ranking is fair as far as it goes and has been truly earned, but they are definitely not qualified either to teach an *art* or to further its progress. What can we do about them? It is impossible at this stage to alter them to any great degree. The solution lies in the future. It must be made more difficult for teachers to be qualified with an Academy blessing, a school certificate should be a minimum requirement and education should include a knowledge of pedagogy, anatomy, physiology and the arts that make up ballet. It is on these lines that the Royal Academy is now working with its recently inaugurated teachers' training course. It may take a generation for the result to be generally noticeable, but then it should be rapid. Meanwhile, the more publicity that can be given to the need in dancers of a cultural background the better, whether they are on the stage or in the classroom. Some of Miss Hopjump's sisters are intelligent; there are public libraries, concerts and lectures available in every centre to-day.

But there are worse problems by far. There is the fifteen-year-old who has passed an exam or so that makes her a member of the Academy, and who starts to teach on the strength of it. The fact that this is not a teacher's certificate is not realised by the general public, who are more or less impressed by any initials after a name. One would imagine that under no circumstances would any parent entrust her child to so young a teacher. Not at all; such teachers exist and they do not lack pupils. Perhaps whatever we do they will continue to exist; doubtless without what they have picked up from the Academy syllabus they would do far greater harm, but it cannot be made too clear that they act with the strong disapproval of all who understand either the ballet or teaching. A partial remedy would be to make any title of membership impossible until a later age. A ten-year-old "member," even when we know what this implies, scarcely adds to the dignity of the body. That is a question of nomenclature, but an all-important one that calls for prompt action. Here again wide publicity is necessary to put down an evil that will grow with the popularity of ballet.

iv. *Examination Pros and Cons*

This leads us on to the whole question of examinations and their value. The great dancer may say, "I never went in for an exam in my life; So-and-so did and passed it with honours. She is in my *corps-de-ballet.*" That has obviously nothing at all to do with the matter. Your great dancer has invariably been taught by a great teacher. We are not concerned with greatness at the moment but with the average person taught by the average teacher. Examinations are essential for both, since there is no other known method of checking results, and an Academy must continually check its results. Its concern is always with the average. It recognises the great artist, exam or no exam.

The examination system is the very best way in which the public can find protection against the fraud; that alone is a full justification.

Exams then are necessary and even beneficial, if properly understood. They very seldom are and consequently their abuse has become something of a danger. I have, in my lecture on *The Making of a Dancer*, drawn the attention of the pupil to this matter. It bears both repetition and amplification. The dancing examination can only be a test of technique and taken as such it is a useful guide to technical progress. *A pupil may pass her advanced examination without being a dancer at all. The teacher must make this point quite plain from the start.* An advanced exam is not a final goal; on the contrary it is the beginning of the freedom necessary for full artistic expression. The Royal Academy of Dancing must not be considered primarily as an examination board. Its examinations are merely a system of accountancy that allow it to strike a balance-sheet of progress. Its main aims will certainly not be understood by the pupil but they are constructive and far-reaching. Whether Mary fails or passes with honours is but an incident, that is too much to expect Mary to understand at the time.

Whether examiners should be teachers with schools of their own is another matter. Obviously they do not examine their own pupils and are scrupulously honest in their decisions. But the functions of teacher and examiner and their interests are so diverse that it would obviously be more in the interests of the art to have an examining board entirely apart. That is an important point that needs underlining. An examining body must be entirely above suspicion, entirely removed from the politics inseparable from every highly competitive profession. An examiner must never be in the position either of taking or turning down as a pupil one of the candidates she has examined. Conscientious teachers do not in fact poach pupils, but they must not even be suspected of the possibility of doing so. An examining board should be like Cæsar's wife.

v. *Ballet* versus *Musical Gym or Worse*

It is an extraordinary thing that our educational schools should be so backward in the teaching of harmonious movement, although the sad case of Miss Hopjump provides one of the main reasons. Even so, the wholesale adoption of a system borrowed from Germany[1] and born of the German defeat in 1919 is a little difficult to understand. This so-called system has little to recommend it from a scholastic point of view ; it is musically unsound, it lacks the necessary discipline and it makes for tightness and bunched muscles rather than for freedom and harmony. Some of its professors are, in the true Germanic manner, clever jugglers with words ; they have assembled a fearsome and to me unintelligible jargon to describe the obvious. I even believe that they have succeeded in deceiving themselves ; a very charitable thought. This lack of discipline—not to be confused with freedom—these heavy, depressed movements, awaken instincts altogether unsuitable in any girl's education. The thing is easy to learn and before the war a brief

[1] With great tact it was styled Central European.

course in Vienna or Berlin provided some sort of qualification, but it is high time that the educational authorities called its bluff.

What is the alternative? Ballet proper?

We are dealing here with the once-a-week child who is not intended for the stage; we are dealing with part of a general education and we must not lose sight of that fact. To start a once-a-week girl on ballet proper as if for an extended career, while far less of an evil than the German (or so called "modern") dance, would not be educationally sound. She would, so to speak, spend her entire time doing scales and would leave school before she had ever played a tune. The essence of the dance as part of general education is: (*a*) its correct relationship to music; (*b*) the training of the body to move harmoniously and therefore healthily; (*c*) the combination of a discipline with the chance of self-expression; (*d*) the possibility of its being linked with the rest of the education. Ballet has just this type of education to offer in what one might call the pre-ballet phase of training.[1] Physically it insists on a correct stance, on freedom of movement and on correct breathing. It develops both sides of musical interpretation, the emotional and the reasoned. It is character-forming, since it calls for memory, the making of quick decisions and for ordered thinking. It is linked both with geography and history through the use of folk and period dances that require a background for their correct rendering.

It is not for me here to outline such a syllabus; that has now been done by experts. Many thoughtful teachers have evolved their own along these lines and have been using it with success

[1] We are, and we always shall be, behind the Central European schools in this question of nomenclature. It was a stroke of genius as far as salesmanship was concerned to have invented the title "modern dance." Pre-ballet training explains what is required to members of the profession but is quite meaningless to the layman, as is also "ballet-based training." We may not escape without a long explanatory title, such as "a system of dance based on ballet and suitable for schools of general education." But then the ballet-mind ever since Noverre and Blasis has set a high value on the precise meaning of words unlike the dance-philosophers of Berlin and Vienna.
A. L. H.

for years. The majority unfortunately have yet to realise that ballet has anything to offer to the school child. That returns us to the Academy teacher's course; every single topic will lead us in that direction.

vi. *A Word in the Ear of the Headmistress*

I have not spared the often well-meaning but not sufficiently qualified dancing teacher; a word now to the headmistress.

Ballet once had a frivolous connotation. True, that was only for a brief period, but it may well be a period that made an impression on you. In its history it has earned the interest and respect of many great minds, Isaac Vossius, Molière and Voltaire among them. It has produced its own great academicians, Noverre and Carlo Blasis, whose works would be of great practical interest to you. Ballet and toe-dancing were once almost synonymous; that is no longer so. You may not like dancing on the toes. We need not argue the point since we are all agreed that the tips of the toes do not enter into our school syllabus. To-day in Britain, dancing, like its sister arts, has its Royal Academy, which has two complementary sides; the one to develop stage dancing as an art for the professional, the other to train and qualify the teacher. You may have been unlucky in the teachers you have met. I sympathise, as you can see. But your alternative is an evil in itself. Dancing cannot be thought of either as gym with music or as a muscle-bound leaping to percussion. We left all that behind us in the jungle. Examine what we have to offer, discuss it with your doctor and your music mistress, give us your advice on this whole question of the fitting of dancing into a curriculum. To-day many of your girls whom I have met are thinking of ballet as a career. You will have seen not only that they have nothing to unlearn but that they have a really splendid start.

vii. *Ballet Clubs and their Role in the Education of the Dancer*

A new feature in the dancing world is the Ballet Club[1] which, if properly understood, has a very big role to play, not only in the appreciation but in the practice of ballet. The Ballet Club is related to the Dramatic or the Operatic Society but with this all-important difference: it must create its own works as well as interpret them. An early pioneer was the Liverpool Ballet Club which consisted of a committee of non-dancers that called on the teachers in the vicinity for their help, and that mounted not only creations of considerable merit but that performed revivals with the co-operation of members of Sadler's Wells. This was an ideal club that for a number of reasons has not yet been imitated. I hope that it will be revived now that the war is over. There are flourishing clubs in Edinburgh, Manchester, Birmingham, Oxford, Cambridge and in many other cities. Their annual programme consists of many other activities besides actual production. Manchester, for instance, has a weekly programme of sketching classes, dancing classes, gramophone recitals and lectures. A ballet club's success depends on the liaison between dancers and musicians and painters.[2] Edinburgh has already made some really important discoveries of decorative artists. Nearly all the clubs, however, are weak on the musical liaison side. London has a similar foundation, the Production Club, an offspring and protégé of the Royal Academy of Dancing. The war prevented the full use of this club, but its possible importance is obvious. Linked in some fashion to the Ballet Clubs all over the country it can arrange for the interchange of productions and guest artistes and can give the provinces a London platform and a fresh and possibly more critical audience. It can spot and help to develop talent in choreography, dancing, music and painting.

[1] The Ballet Club movement should not be confused with Marie Rambert's remarkable venture of that name with its headquarters at the Mercury Theatre. Hers is, of course, a fully professional company.

[2] See lecture to Ballet Clubs, page 79.

The scarcity in ballet is not one of dancers but of choreographers. It is obviously impossible for economic reasons for a large company to risk being too experimental. The Ballet Club movement gives just such an opportunity. Properly used it is ideal for the further education of the teacher and the dancer. Its lectures alone provide an admirable night-school programme. In many cases it can take the place of the school show, providing far greater resources, and it can most certainly prove a substitute for many of those damaging pot-hunting, jealousy-inspiring competitions. The young dancer needs some stage experience ; that is the argument used by the apologist for competitions. Well, here is the chance of such experience under conditions that are far closer to the professional stage. And not the least of the triumphs of the Ballet Club movement will be to bring the dancing teacher, the painter and the musician together round the committee-room table.

The musician is still a little shy of the whole thing, and he is wrong. Dancers have played havoc with music ; they always will until he lends his support. He will then find ballet an admirable medium that will give him an opportunity to compose or arrange music, to conduct or to play under theatre conditions. The Ballet Club belongs as much to the college of music and the art school as it does the dancing school. I hope that the dancers and their admirers who are the leading spirits in the movement will make this fact quite clear.

viii. *Dancing as a Career : Some Difficulties*

We have looked at the cases of the education of the dancing teacher and the position of dancing in the general curriculum. What of the case of the girl who intends to take up ballet as a career ? Not the least interesting part of my tour was the many talks I had with parents, school teachers and the girls themselves. It is obvious that the girl requires the time to attend her dancing class. I had been warned by several parents that schools were definitely hostile and that it had become a question of education or career. This as a general rule was not at all the case as far as the day school was concerned. Where the dancing teacher in any district was a serious person I found the headmistress interested and most eager to help. In three cases headmistresses sent for the girls so that I could see and advise them. The headmistress wanted to be convinced that this was a serious career. Rightly she felt it her duty to protect the girl. In general she was not willing to allow time off for entry into some pot-hunting, tap-cum-ballet competition ; but Royal Academy examinations were an entirely different matter. I have no doubt, though I have never happened to meet them, that there are prejudiced headmistresses, but in the main the problem lies with us. The Royal Academy of Dancing has it in its power to clear up all doubts and misunderstandings. My experience shows me that once the headmistress is convinced that the girl's vocation is real and the teaching likely to advance it, she will help in every way possible. At present it is the fine work shown by Sadler's Wells on its tours and the personality of Ninette de Valois that has done more to convince scholastic authorities than anything else.

The boarding-school presents different and far more difficult problems. I have recently received letters from boarding-schools in the heart of the country and there was no immediate solution because the distances were too far for a visiting teacher. This will only solve itself when there are dancing teachers capable of becoming resident members of a school staff, teaching the ballet-based dance to the school and ballet proper to the specialists. A few such schools do exist ; one in particular has made a noted success.

On several occasions I came across girls eager to take up dancing who were encountering strong parental opposition. In one case the girl was laid up with a nervous breakdown. At the request of sympathetic headmistresses I interviewed these girls. The headmistress was prepared to intervene, if I found that the girl had a future. It so happened that in every case they were physically unsuited to be dancers, which will of course happen nine times out of ten. Had the parents adopted the only reasonable attitude and let the girls find out for themselves there would have been no sense of frustration. After our interview one of the girls was fully reconciled to becoming a doctor as her parents wished ; another to go to the University to study with a view to becoming a teacher. The girl with a nervous breakdown had by then become a far more complicated problem. The parents had caused real damage.

I think that the opposite case is even more frequent ; the mother who urges on her unwilling daughter because she herself was thwarted in a desire to go on the stage and wants all the excitement of such a life, even at second hand. Every teacher knows that type of parent and will, I hope, have as little patience with her as I have. Another dangerous parent is the one who says, " Your Father and I have made great sacrifices to have you taught dancing, now you must go out and earn some money and help us." As the unfortunate girl is usually but a month or two above school-leaving age this is nothing short of exploitation.

I have long been used to the " theatre-mamma " and her little ways ; the " classroom mamma " is equally bad. In no other lesson would the mother walk in and watch, but with dancing she takes it as her right. Even if she is thoroughly well meaning, her very presence upsets the teacher-pupil relationship. The teacher has to understand her mothers and deal with them for the good of the pupils. The very first thing is to keep them out of the classroom. " Do you walk into the arithmetic lesson ? " I heard one strong-minded teacher ask. Her results were so obviously first-class that she carried the day.

Those then are still more of the difficulties that the teacher of dancing has to face in preparing her pupils for a stage career.

Is it surprising that I should demand a really fine type, morally courageous, well educated and a true teacher by vocation, as the final product of the Royal Academy of Dancing?

ix. *Conclusion: A Real Opportunity*

This survey of the dancing profession may seem a depressing one and it may be thought that I should have kept the matter for family discussion. I disagree. There are, fortunately for the writer, many thousands who are interested in reading books about ballet. It is high time that they had a peep behind the scenes. Publicity in such matters can do nothing but good. Parents, school-children, teachers, dancing teachers and, more remotely, future audiences are all involved and each one has a role to play.

Dance teaching in this country is, with some magnificent exceptions, on an alarmingly low level, technically, artistically and in its relationship to culture in general. The Royal Academy of Dancing is in the unique position of being able to solve these problems one by one. It has all the prestige of its charter and possesses the necessary experts to bring these things about. Time is now short because this is a period of great change in education. The Academy must be vigorous; it must not be afraid of upsetting some of the more stubbornly backward teachers. Indeed, it must forget that it ever was a teachers' association. To act as an examining board is but one of its functions. An Academy must set a technical and artistic standard and reject all those unwilling and unable to conform. Only in that way will it play the very great role which is expected of it and which it is well able to fulfil

THE MAKING OF A DANCER

AND OTHER PAPERS ON THE BALLET

The original lectures

dedicated to

IRENE HAMMOND
FREDERIC and VALERIE LLOYD
W. J. TURNER
MARJORY MIDDLETON
CÊCILE WALTON
MOLLIE RADCLIFFE

AND THE AUTHOR'S FRIENDS
AT THE EDINBURGH BALLET CLUB

whose kindness to the lecturer has made a pleasure of his many long journeys

I

THE MAKING OF A DANCER

I FEEL that as the dancers and teachers of the future you form by far my most important audience, yet we are often sadly at cross-purposes. You have a tendency to think of dancing in terms of steps performed efficiently, while in watching you I want to forget all about steps and to see the dance as a whole. It is because of that particular viewpoint that I am going to talk to you about the dancer as an artiste, for when I use the term " dancer " that is what I mean.

Let us first take a look at the finished product ; a Pavlova, supreme artiste in movement, holding us spellbound not necessarily in some great work but " in the dance of every day danced as no one had ever danced it before," to quote a great artiste, Alexandre Benois. See how she folds her petals in *The Californian Poppy*, how enchanting the simple *pas de bourrée* becomes in her drama of *The Dying Swan*. Now look at a Karsavina, supreme in a great work, surrounded by a great company, infinitely versatile as the tragedy queen in *Thamar* or the innocent young girl in *Spectre de la Rose*. Take the President of our Academy, Adeline Genée, the embodiment of porcelain grace, meticulous in technique but always subordinating that technique so that it serves her, revealing intelligence in her every movement. You are too young to have seen those dancers, though you should know of them, so I will end by quoting a young contemporary, Margot Fonteyn, our one undisputed ballerina, who builds up each role with a rare intelligence, who interprets music, whose dancing forms a connected whole. All these widely differing personalities have many things in common. You will see what they are as I proceed.

Now let us go to the other extreme, from the sublime to

the domestic, and imagine a familiar family scene. Mother and father are sitting in their parlour ; small daughter is improvising a dance to the wireless. Father—and it usually is father—turns to mother and says, " Look at her, isn't she graceful, a regular Pavlova. We must have her taught dancing." Many of you must have started in that way, possibly because your parents had been watching some great dancer the previous night. From London to Sydney, from New York to Shanghai, Pavlova inspired parents. Three-quarters of the young dancers of de Basil's company owed their start to her influence.

We are immediately confronted by the first problem—what school to choose. Now in France, Russia or Denmark the matter is comparatively simple. There are state academies for the very talented, while the others have a choice of teachers turned out by those academies and who teach according to a known standard. In this country it is different. Anyone who can raise the funds to hire a room and can put up a shiny brass plate—that is essential—with the words " teacher," or better still, " professor of dancing " on it can open a school. It is the same with music, elocution or drawing, but in those cases, apart from the waste of money and talent, no serious damage is done. In dancing it is different ; grave physical damage can be caused, fallen arches, deformed limbs and worse. I see such signs all too often, though things are growing better. That is where our Academy comes in. It is a magnificent British compromise, just as C.E.M.A., to-day the Arts Council of Great Britain, is a compromise for a Ministry of Fine Arts. It respects the private teacher and gives both her and her pupils magnificent advantages. Through its exams it guarantees a high level of safety. The work of a Royal Academy teacher has been inspected by a competent authority and the syllabus very carefully and skilfully drawn up.

Let us say then that our imaginary pupil is now learning her five positions under the watchful eye of a Royal Academy member. Now in her future education there are three partners

—her dancing teacher, her mother and her school teacher. The dancing teacher's role is obvious, but apart from teaching you dance steps she requires a mature judgment, a knowledge of psychology; for remember, she is dealing with individual cases and not turning out utility dancers on a mass production belt.

A familiar motto says that a girl's best friend is her mother. If you had travelled, as I have, with a ballet company, accompanied by fourteen mothers, you might very well doubt the truth of that. Indeed, I always say, "God protect me from dancing mothers." I will assume, for safety's sake, that there are none of that type in your city; but in other cities mothers all too often bring pressure on the dancing teacher to hurry up the whole process. They have developed a pot-hunting attitude and think only of winning prizes in competitions. These mothers are thwarted dancers. Their one ambition is to have their unfortunate girls photographed on the tips of their wobbling toes, grinning idiotically and surrounded by cups and medals. The wise teacher will not listen, but it does impose a strain.

The role of the last partner, the schoolmistress, is as yet too little recognised. There is no room on the stage for the ill-educated girl. Yet how often do we hear, "She's going to be a dancer, so she doesn't need any education." Those great dancers of the past, products of state academies, all had educations that carried them well beyond our school certificate standard. Without such an education this is what happens. Your immature dancer delights her audience for a while. She is young and enthusiastic; art and play are not so far apart. Then she begins to develop mannerisms and soon we forget her in our eagerness to applaud the next child prodigy. A child's instinct, so often right, can only be replaced by reason. We need the co-operation of the schoolmistress, especially with the raising of the school age, but we shall only get it when we are able to convince her that we ourselves regard dancing as a serious art. So stick to your school books.

We have left our young pupil at the *barre*, doubtless sticking her tongue out with every fresh problem she meets—it is wonderful what a great role the tongue plays with the embryo dancer.

The first matters to be considered are physical. To succeed as an artiste the dancer requires physical beauty. I see some of you glancing at the mirror, and, as I don't want to spread alarm and despondency, let me explain myself. This has nothing to do with pin-up girls or Betty Grable. It is a good deal more subtle. The films, and Hollywood in particular, have perverted all our ideals of beauty. They take character and individuality and turn out so many dolls. The beauty I mean is a part of the stagecraft and training of the actress, whether beautiful in fact or not, to be able to convince the majority of her audience that she is beautiful. In your case there is yet another reason. As a dancer your body is as assuredly your instrument as the violin is Kreisler's ; a Stradivarius greatly improves the quality of a performance. He could not impress his audience, master though he is, on a cigar-box fiddle ; neither could you with a squint or knock-knees. But there is a more hopeful side suggested to me by those words knock-knees. A ballerina, whose name is a household word to-day, first took up ballet on her doctor's advice to cure a bad case of knock-knees. From a remedial point of view ballet technique, scientifically taught, can perform wonders in creating harmony, mental as well as physical. Only recently I heard of a case of a child in a primary school in a very poor district. She was undersized, unkempt, bad at games and work and unpopular. Her headmistress, an understanding woman, asked her if she had any ambition. The child immediately answered " to be a ballerina." The headmistress wrote to ask me about a school and sent the girl, paying out of her own pocket. The last letter I received a few weeks ago says, " She has passed her elementary R.A.D., just missing honours by a mark, but that is not the most important. The whole change in her is striking. She is tidy, much more enterprising in her schoolwork and really popular with the other girls. She is now average size." Such cases are not exceptional.

The next thing to be dealt with is this vexed question of technique. I call it a vexed question because so many of you dancers seem to misunderstand its whole meaning and purpose and to worship it, a truly hideous idol. I have just read a very significant criticism of a well-known dancer: "Pavlova sacrificed technique for personality while Mlle. X. has sacrificed her personality for technique." I call that damning. The result of technique-worship is not only that many of you will never become dancers at all, but that by misunderstanding the whole thing you give weapons to the opponents of ballet—and there are many, usually far more thoughtful people than the ballet dancers and their admirers.

They see our small pupil struggling with her exercises and say, "You see how stiff, rigid and unimaginative she has become. She used to dance quite spontaneously once." As a result they recommend some form of alleged "natural" dancing, skipping about on bare feet, pretending to be a bird or a butterfly, or, far worse, this cavorting to drum or gong, for some odd reason styled "the modern dance," which is in fact neither modern nor dancing.

The way to answer their misunderstanding and yours is to quote the more familiar case of the pianist. You all know those charming people who can strum by ear, greatly to their own delight and to that of uncritical friends in the noisy social atmosphere of the club-room or canteen. Teach these care-free strummers to read music, and for some time the result will be scales and exercises. Once those have been mastered and only then will the pianist be really free to interpret music. Technique is merely machinery, the machinery you set into motion in order to *create* a work of art, a poem, a painting, or to *interpret* a work of art on an instrument; and your body is an instrument. Technique is a means and not an end. How often Diaghileff repeated that phrase. Do not be pleased when people praise your technique, it shows that they have nothing more flattering to mention. Do not imagine that because some of you have passed an advanced exam you are necessarily dancers. To do so would be to misunderstand the whole purpose of our very valuable exams. They are milestones in education : they provide a method of concentrating work. They may be an immediate goal : they can never be an ultimate aim ; that is, if it is your aim to be an artiste. Remember, that to acquire complete freedom technique is indispensable and freedom of expression is the only thing to work for in the dance studio. A *pas de bourrée*, however perfect, is not a thing to wonder at. Pavlova's *Dying Swan* was.

I sometimes wonder if the education of the general public, your future audience, in the technique of the dance is not a very harmful thing. They do so love talking of *fouettés* and *cabrioles* that they tend to lose sight completely of the dance as a whole.

Now let us leave the purely physical to consider your relationship to the arts. You will need the partnership of music, drama and painting to add to your dancing before you can take your place in ballet.

Music is the first of the arts that you meet. It inspired you when you improvised to that wireless. Now the focus has shifted and instead of inspiration it has become a mathematical guide—" One, two, one, two—listen to the beat. Mary you're out of time again." How I pity your class and rehearsal pianists. I feel also that we have not done enough for you yet in our selection of music for class purposes. This wholesale murder of portions of the classics is a deplorable beginning to your artistic education. To listen to music for the beat is a basic requirement, it is our old friend the tom-tom in the Kaffir kraal. There are other important relationships too often neglected. You must feel the music and you must understand the music, if you are to interpret it in addition to merely keeping time. Pavlova's feeling for music, quite apart from any intellectual understanding of it, was one of the secrets of her art. There was a Pavlova mystery which I never understood while she lived. I had to write of her performances. They moved me deeply, but there was so little to get hold of—often poor music, weak dances, pretty costumes. I was reduced to using very long words. Always beware of critics who use long words; it is a sure sign that they don't understand what they are writing about. It was only after her death when, in company with a famous conductor, I saw films of her dancing that I really understood. He was there to synchronise those films to sound. They had been taken by amateurs without any musical accompaniment. The conductor was openly sceptical, but when the film began his amazement was intense: "She has the whole orchestra in her body, every subtlety of accent and phrasing." The old poet was right when he said that the great dancer is borne aloft on the arms of the music. That is an inborn gift; it can be developed by good teaching and killed by bad. Pavlova had little intellectual understanding of music. She refused to dance *The Firebird* which was written with her in mind. You can develop an intellectual understanding of music and the piano is a very important part of your complete education. A knowledge of piano gave our great English dancer Sokolova a chance in Russian Ballet as early as 1912. She was able to master the then difficult rhythm of Ravel's *Daphnis and Chloe* and so gained her first step on the ladder.

The dancer's ignorance of music is a byword with musicians. Only three weeks ago I came upon a dancer who had taken two waltzes of Chopin, rid himself of what he called "the unnecessary portions" and telescoped them. He—and it was a he this time—was very pleased with himself. I like to think that this was an extreme case, but your cuts and repeats have made many a composer turn in his grave. Learn as much music as you can and when in doubt, both dancers and teachers, always take expert advice. Musicians are sympathetic to the dance and will be still more so when we treat their art with due respect.

The next art you will meet, though you may not always know it, is the art of drama. Let me first of all correct a wrong impression that is all too common. Acting for the dancer does not consist in a series of carefully studied faces labelled *hate*, *fear*, *love* and then stuck into a dance. It is a part of the dance, and your eyebrows are as much a concern of the dance as your toes. Fokine laid down that the dancer must be expressive from head to foot. Take his *Les Sylphides* ; that too is a problem in acting though it has no story. Your problem here is to suggest an atmosphere, nymphs in a wood. How are you going to tackle it ? If you are acting Ophelia or Lady Macbeth, you start at any rate by knowing what it is all about. In *Les Sylphides* there is no book of reference that can possibly tell you how nymphs behave, either in or out of woods. There is only one answer : you must listen to the music, *there* is your book, your only dramatic guide. We are back at music again. We shall never leave it for long.

Mime in ballet is a different matter. It is a type of sign language that very few dancers can perform with conviction at the present day. The acting or narrative part of contemporary ballet is not a separate thing but a part of the dance as whole.

Now let me give you a tip. At some time or other you will all have to make up a *demi-caractère* dance for an exam or one of those loathsome competitions. First let us be clear about *demi-caractère*. You use your orthodox technique to express or suggest some character, let us say a Columbine as in *Carnaval*. The usual method is to hunt about for the character in a fairy book or book of folklore. When you have found your idea you have another search ahead of you. " What music can I find for ' Penelope spinning ' ? " It is both difficult and dangerous to fit already composed music to a library idea ; we have seen one young dancer's solution in the unfortunate case of the telescoping of Chopin. I suggest that you let your body do the thinking through improvisation to the right type of light music. Movement will come, followed by some idea of the character, and the search is at an end. You have the appropriate music ; you started with it.

This improvisation is an admirable thing ; don't leave it behind in the nursery. It is more than ever important when your mind and body are weary with technical problems. It contains the germ of choreography. All choreographers have started with their own bodies. A word of warning here. Please don't strive after originality when you arrange your dances. A charming Bo-peep is worth all the pretentious Spirits of Progress, and Miss Muffet infinitely preferable to a misfiring aeroplane. If you are original, it will certainly emerge; if you aren't, aim at doing the everyday thing supremely well.

Our last arts in this ballet partnership are the plastic arts of painting and sculpture. You have all heard people say " Mary wears a costume well, Joan wears a costume badly." What does it mean ? Surely they both have hips on which to hang the costume !

In dancing your costume is a part of you. That is so much the case that our whole dance technique has developed with the history of costume. You must learn that history. Ballet first grew up at Court. Dresseswere long and stately, touching the ground, so that the dance could only be a pattern along the ground. Then Camargo shortened the skirt, revealing the ankles, and the *batterie* was developed. Later, with the invention of theatre tights, the body was free for the modern virtuoso technique. In the older dance, the legs and feet being hidden, the accent was on the arms and body ; later it shifted to the legs, and dancing was mistakenly held to mean leg movements alone.

A study of art is therefore indispensable, if you are to understand style, if you are to wear your costumes well. The museums and picture galleries are an encyclopædia of poses. Greek and Gothic sculpture, renaissance and baroque are all intimately bound up with our art. Your lovely *attitude*, for instance, was taken from Jan Bologna's Mercury. Noverre and Carlo Blasis, great architects of ballet, had an encyclopædic knowledge of painting and sculpture, as did Diaghileff, Benois and Fokine who gave us our contemporary ballet, the art in which you will take your place. If your aim is teaching and not the stage, what I have to say is even more important.

Try to draw a dancer ; the sense of line required whether in drawing or in your own bodies is very much the same. I have seen very interesting work by dancers from Pavlova downwards, and the thought required will teach you a great deal. If later you aspire to choreography, such knowledge will be of the greatest value.

All that I have said may discourage you, by making the road between steps and true dancing seem a long and arduous one. It is, but you should not be discouraged. No art worth acquiring is easy and you have a true mission to perform. Our academy is the youngest of all the art academies. To the unthinking there is still the suggestion of something frivolous about dancing your way through life. So many things are called dancing, so many people dabble. Voltaire loved ballet because it was a science with strict rules as well as an art. You must justify that saying by your whole attitude towards your work, and to-day your chances are many. There are British companies in search of talent, foreign companies that will look increasingly to British dancers—a recent one was a hundred per cent. British—and the development of television will bring dancers a rich harvest. Our President, Madame Genée, was a pioneer in television. I was in the studio when she made an appearance in 1934, in the old experimental days when she had to wear a heavy clown-like mask of make-up.

Yes, things will move swiftly now and the image of your dancing will be carried to many a country cottage or farmhouse parlour. Good-bye, and good luck to you all.

II

WHAT IS BALLET?

I WONDER whether you ever realise what an important role you as an audience have to play? The performance can ultimately only be as good as you wish it to be. That is the very great difference with the cinema, where there is a machine in place of flesh and blood and a considerable time-lag between you and the actual performance. If you stayed away it might, through that sensitive instrument the box-office, convince those hard- or perhaps soft-headed business men who control the films that something was wrong, though they would never really know what that something was. But then you do not stay away because, unfortunately, in your city there is so little else to do for entertainment. People in Great Britain and America are rapidly forgetting what it means to be an audience.

I have never forgotten something that Pavlova told me at Covent Garden. She had just danced her wonderful *Dying Swan*. Her audience was yelling itself hoarse, shouting, clapping and stamping. She turned to me and said, "I do wish they hadn't given me such an ovation to-night. I know I wasn't dancing well, and I shall lose all my standards if they behave so uncritically."

The fine artiste deserves a critical audience. To-day in this country we have a great national ballet company, Sadler's Wells. It is doing remarkable work in making known to the world, and to ourselves, that we are a creative nation artistically. Your share in its work is to be critical and to know something of the medium in which it is working. Ballet is an exceedingly delicate art that soon suffers when it is not understood and that through such misunderstanding has already once in its distinguished history found itself in the music hall, sandwiched in between the performing seal and the juggler—not that I despise seals and jugglers; they were often far more artistic than the ballet.

Let me begin by warning you that this is a delayed-action lecture; you may not enjoy it to-night, but I do hope that it will enable you to enjoy the ballet more next time.

The first thing to realise about ballet is that it is not an art on its own but an equal partnership between the arts of dancing, painting, music and drama; a tapestry, if you like, in which if you pull away one of the threads, the whole thing comes to pieces. I am going to examine those threads one by one and to show you the role that each plays in the lovely pattern that is ballet.

The first of our arts is dancing, oldest of them all, oldest form of self-expression known to mankind. Some ballet dancers and their more unthinking fans will try to convince you that ballet dancing and dancing are for all practical purposes exactly the same thing. They are wrong, of course. They are denying the whole history of their art. If the whole history of dancing were written in ten mighty volumes—which would in fact amount to a social history of mankind—ballet would occupy at most a single chapter. Ballet is a modern, Western European, theatrical form of dancing. It requires an audience, where the folk or the social dance do not. You are that audience. Ballet, as we know it, originated at the court of King Louis XIV in France. It was made up of the dances of courtiers, peasants and the acrobats and tumblers from the fair grounds. Its technique and artistry were developed in succeeding generations by certain great exponents such as Noverre and Blasis whose writings are still of importance to-day. All this is not merely a dry bit of history but is extremely practical. It means that while ballet technique is modern and European, the ballet producer has the movement of the whole world from its youth to the present day to draw upon for his inspiration and material. That brings us at once to this vexed question of technique. Let me try and situate it right away. *Ballet technique is a system of physical educa-*

tion that enables the dancer to be expressive in every type of movement. If dancers would only understand that simple proposition, what a difference it would make to their art.

I must shift now from the dancer on the stage to you in the audience. If, when you visit the ballet, you turn to your neighbour in the interval and say, "Isn't La Smithova a remarkable technical dancer," you prove two things: her technique is inadequate and she is certainly no artiste. Technique is no concern of yours in the audience. It must be sufficient for the dancer to be completely free to express what is in the dance. If that is the case, then it is good technique. Pavlova never had a wide range of mechanical tricks and some years before she died she simplified her dances, drastically in some cases. The public never noticed; she moved them as greatly as ever. I remember sitting with Pavlova, watching a small child turning an extraordinary number of *fouettés*. She turned to me and said, "I have never been able to do anything of the kind." But that did not mean that the child was a better dancer, even from the purely technical point of view. I usually underline this by giving the example of two girls performing the same sequence of steps to the same music; one will be an acrobat, the other a dancer.

Take our acrobat first. She listens to the music for guidance in tempo; then the whole object of her dance is to convince you that what she is doing is very difficult. She stresses all her preparations—"now I am going to turn . . . watch me carefully . . . now I am going to do a brilliant series of beats," and so on. She ends up with a tremendous climax. She gains applause for the good old reason of difficulty overcome. This is so much the case that if, in the middle of her dance, she falls on her behind, raising a cloud of dust, when she gets up to resume the dance she will be greeted with frantic applause. Let me add that that is merely because we are such a sporting nation. It has nothing to do with art.

Now for our true dancer, something of a rarity at all times.

She listens to the music, not only for guidance in tempo but for its content. Her concern is with interpretation. Consequently she makes everything appear natural and easy. She will very possibly not get half the applause at the finish but she may get this very remarkable tribute, a fraction of a second of dead silence before the applause. Only the very greatest receive that silence, as if the audience were frightened of breaking a spell.

While we are on the subject of ballet technique let us turn our attention to one of its greatest opponents, Isadora Duncan. Now it is possible to be a great dancer without having received a single dancing lesson ; possible though infinitely rare. And Duncan at her best was a very great dancer. But certain consequences follow : she was uneven from night to night, there were many blanks in her dances where inspiration failed, and when she was no longer young unlike Pavlova she presented a truly pathetic spectacle. She had no technique to tell her about herself. Most important of all from the point of view of the continuity of the dance, her art was so strictly personal that once Duncan was no more there could be no Duncanism. The interesting and important thing is that Duncan's influence survives in the ballet that she disliked so intensely. And it will always be so. An art with an academic technique can survive periods when inspiration is lacking and take new strength to itself when inspiration returns. It has the power of attracting to itself all sorts of outside influences. There is the case of Duncan yesterday : to-day the central Europeans of the Wigman-Laban type have had a certain definite influence on ballet while their own form of dancing was a mushroom growth without a future. That is the value of a precise technique.

And look what it can accomplish in practice. The same company can perform *The Swan Lake* in strict accordance with ballet technique ; *Daphnis and Chloe* in the Greek idiom and on bare feet ; *Le Sacre du Printemps*, modern primitive of the most advanced type ; *The Three Cornered Hat* in the Spanish folk idiom ;

and the *Miracle in the Gorbals*, a drama set in the slums. Ballet technique does not keep the dancer within narrow limits : on the contrary it gives her a scope that no other system could possibly allow. That is the answer to the critics of ballet, the final answer. Only I wish I could be certain that all dancers really understood it and did not mistake the technical means for the artistic end.

The second of our arts is music and we have already seen how great a role its correct understanding played when we talked of the difference between dancer and acrobat. The primitive relationship between music and dancing is purely one of rhythmic accompaniment ; the modern one is so close that the dancing might almost be called visual music. The aim of a Duncan was the interpretation of music, a conception that ballet had forgotten when she was at the height of her fame. It has always seemed strange to me that she took her main inspiration from ancient Greece via the sculpture and paintings on vases, which in themselves reveal no movement and which were not literal transcriptions but a part of the vase or carving on which they were depicted. To achieve a real Greek dance it is essential for us to know something of Greek music, which is a sealed book. This means that she limited herself very severely in the scope of her musical interpretation, all of which brings us back once again to technique. I drew your attention to how very closely the elements of ballet are interwoven.

The same thing happens when we discuss drama ; half the time we are talking about music. Drama in ballet is a term that means very much more than the telling in movement of some story, though that is one of the forms that it may take. The very story to be told or character to be sketched depends on the music. The purely literary mind has no place in ballet, though in criticising ballet the *littérateur* often astonishes the dancers by discovering a wealth of meaning in their movements that they did not dream existed. I do hope that I have kept reasonably free from that type of criticism.

It is an interesting thing that the more story there is in a ballet the less the story really matters. The classical ballet such as *Swan Lake* has a long and definite plot, complete with villains, bewitched princesses and all the usual romantic paraphernalia. Although many of you have seen it more than once, I doubt if you could tell me the story correctly. It just doesn't matter. Diaghileff compressed it into one act with no dramatic loss. It was merely a pretext for very beautiful movement to very beautiful music. You can similarly compress any one of these classics with no dramatic loss ; you can put only one act on the programme and no one complains. Fokine was also a romantic in outlook. His *Sylphides* is as romantic in conception as any *Swan Lake*. It has no story whatsoever ; it is just pure romanticism without any of the period paraphernalia. But the interpretation of the *prélude*, for instance, calls for much more than dancing. That is one example of drama in ballet, the suggestion of a particular atmosphere. When the *soliste* fails in this it is invariably as an actress or a musician and never as a technical dancer. Let us go from the prelude of *Les Sylphides* to the other extreme, *The Miracle in the Gorbals*. This is a modern morality ballet, and here the plot is of extreme importance, because without an understanding of it every movement is meaningless and has little of the absolute beauty of its own that depends on line. Here every member of the company is acting some *definite* role the whole time. In *Les Sylphides* the music gives the inspiration direct to the dancer. In *The Miracle in the Gorbals* the relationship alters ; choreographer, dancers and composer are working on a common theme, but that theme is conveyed to the dancers still via the music but only after they have worked out in detail their role in the plot. These things are complex to discuss without actual examples in front of us but they do show the scope of drama in ballet. *The Miracle in the Gorbals* is a striking success because its setting and direct narrative allow it to be told through the dance, but it creates a dangerous precedent full of pitfalls save for the most experienced. The minimum of plot and the more direct relationship between what is heard and what is interpreted should be the general rule.

We now come to the painter's role, which is often greatly misunderstood by the use on the programme of the French word *décors*, which in our sense does not mean decorations or embellishments. In the bad old period of ballet just as any music could be used so long as it had the required rhythm, so could any scenery and costumes be used. Neither belonged to the partnership. Diaghileff altered that position. His costumes and scenery were a definite part of the whole. This meant that the painter had to be familiar with the music and with the type of grouping and movements to be used. His backcloth must fit into that movement. Alter the scenery of a *Schéhérazade* or *Petrouchka* and the whole character of the ballet is changed. Costumes and scenery are usually failures when the painter is called in to dress an already existing work. You will find that many modern ballets have originated in the mind of such painters as Benois, Bakst, Picasso or Derain.

It now remains to deal with an artist whose function is less familiar to the general public and who is described in the programme as the choreographer. He is the man or woman, always a dancer of experience, who creates the actual movement that you see. His task is a difficult one because he has to be familiar with so many arts. He must know ballet and its technique, court and national dancing. He must feel music and understand it technically. He must have a considerable knowledge of sculpture and painting which are the inspiration for much of his grouping and his guide to style. Added to that he must, of course, have something to express. It is not sufficient to make permutations and combinations of the classroom steps. There is no real way in which he can be trained, because it is not easy to procure a company upon which he can practise or experiment. The composer works on paper without an orchestra, this is denied the choreographer. Small wonder that choreographers are scarce; it is something of a marvel that they exist at all. I have seen all the great contemporary choreographers at work. Each one has his individual method of working. Let me give you a few examples. Fokine arrived at the first rehearsal with a ballet that was completely finished in his mind, and put it on as if working on a revival. He expected his dancers to be finished technicians and he explained and demonstrated the dramatic content in detail. Nijinska preferred to work with a group of dancers for some time, to accustom them to her individual style, and she was meticulous about casting. With her choreography came out of the classroom. Ashton conceives in terms of movement; Helpmann in terms of drama; and so on.

There are no rules save knowledge and authority. Dancers need convincing that the choreographer knows his job. If a movement "feels wrong," they will soon show him and too many such cases will destroy the entire work. You must conceive of the choreographer as a man walking on a tight-rope and juggling with plates marked music, pattern, line, colour, drama. Personally I find it much easier to be a critic.

These then are some of the points involved in the making of a ballet. I have tried to point them out to you without using any critical jargon. These are very many others which I deal with in more detail in my other lectures. Bear them in mind when next you visit the ballet, and on your way home ask yourself three simple questions. What did the producer set out to do? Was it worth doing? Has he succeeded? That is the basis of all criticism.

III

BALLET AND MUSIC

There have been no more loathsome importations into the English language than those words *high-brow* and *low-brow* and, of the two, *low-brow* is by far the most obnoxious. How smug the low-brow with that wretched slogan of his, " I don't know much about art, but I do know what I like." Such an attitude will have little sympathy with the members of your Society. In music it leads to that atrocious instrument the cinema organ with its obscene noises, or to the crooner, thin disguise for the bad singer ; in painting it produces the chocolate box, " love among the roses." In ballet it is still more dangerous and when it persisted, although the word low-brow was still fortunately unknown, ballet ceased to interest the serious composer and artiste and found its way to the music-hall, where it appealed to the tired business man.

It is so easy to accept ballet as something beautiful that we can enjoy without effort, and then so easy for the beautiful to become pretty. The serious composer has only been interested in ballet when ballet has been true to itself as a medium. Our concern in this lecture is with music in ballet.

There are three possible relationships between music and the dance ; one of them I will dismiss in a few words. Many dancers have said : " Why should the dance be a slave to music ? Let us free the dance. To do this the music must follow the rhythm of our dancing. We indicate the rhythm, the orchestra follows with the appropriate noises." Serge Lifar, late of the Paris *Opéra*, wrote a very wordy manifesto on this subject and put his idea into practice with a weird but not wholly uninteresting ballet *Icare*. When I remembered that as a dancer he had been conspicuously unmusical I understood what lay behind this fervent plea for freedom. Now this whole argument shows an extraordinary lack of knowledge as to the basic composition of ballet. Ballet, I cannot repeat this too often, is not an art on its own but is made up of the partnership of dance music, drama and the plastic arts, and *partnership* is the operative word. In any period where one of the partners has shone at the expense of the others ballet as a whole has suffered. The supreme test of a good ballet is the delicate relationship between the arts ; each one expressing the same thing in its particular medium. Before the war there was a cry to free the dance from scenery and costume ; that too is luckily a dead issue.

The first feasible relationship between dance and music is the primitive one of stamping feet, clapped hands, shouted chants, the tom-tom. That relationship is older than speech or music ; it came about when man's ancestor first stood erect, when he evoked his gods for success in the hunt or in war. It is strange that this primitive relationship between sound and movement should have been discovered by various Central European professors between the two wars and launched as something novel with a perfect avalanche of long words. Stranger still that it should have found its way under the misleading title of " the modern dance " into the physical training curriculum of many of our schools, where nothing could be more unsuitable physically, psychologically or as education. The fact that it is easy to acquire may have something to do with the choice.

This primitive relationship means that the music exists solely as a rhythmic guide ; the tapping of the ballet master's stick would serve equally well. In ballet's degenerate days after the glories of the romantic period of Taglioni and her peers, and indeed even then, there was a sharp distinction drawn between music and " ballet-music." This " ballet-music " was ordered in bulk, so to speak ; an hour and a half of assorted rhythm with a waltz every twenty minutes for safety. It could be cut up and then joined together with scissors and paste and no harm done. More important still, you could substitute entirely different music, yet as long as it had a similar rhythm the ballet would remain unaltered. This could scarcely be called a partnership of the arts. Even Adolphe Adam's *Giselle*, the only ballet of the Romantic period to survive, is trivial musically. Its rather charming melodies bear little relationship to the mighty drama that unfolds itself. They are certainly of no help to the dancer in her interpretation of the role, so that this inadequacy also upsets the delicate relationship of drama to ballet. Such utility composers as Minkus and Pugno long persisted in ballet. The advent of Tchaikovsky announced a new era. Not only is his music an inspiration to the dancer and his melodies of great beauty in themselves, they are also a complete guide to attack and style. With Tchaikovsky the romantic fairy tale comes alive, he is a Perrault among composers.

This primary relationship which we are still discussing can be disguised, by which I mean that the purpose of the music may still be purely rhythmic but that the music itself may be charmingly ornamented as in the case of a Drigo, for instance.

The contemporary relationship between music and the dance, of which Tchaikovsky represents the *avant garde* and that was ushered in by Duncan, Fokine and Diaghileff, is where not only the rhythm is significant but also the style, character and form. The music in such a case inspires as well as accompanies the dance. It is a true partner in Fokine's sense of the word.

Such "inspirational" music may be commissioned or arranged. The ideal is music especially written with a definite ballet in mind and where the partners work together from the very beginning. Conspicuous among such partnerships are the cases of Tchaikovsky and Petipa, Stravinsky and Fokine and, more recently, Lambert and Ashton in *Horoscope* and Bliss and Helpmann in *The Miracle of the Gorbals*. During the recent visit of Sadler's Wells to Paris the first thing the critics noted was that in their use of music the British company came closest to the Diaghileff ideal; and French critics have always understood ballet as a whole. But for obvious reasons commissioned music must be the exception rather than the rule. Modern companies travel a great deal too much for their good and the close association between artistes that was the rule in Diaghileff's Monte Carlo is no longer possible. For instance, the ballet to William Walton's recent *Quest*, a most distinguished score, was created under great war-time difficulties and one can feel that the Ashton-Walton partnership was less complete than it should have been, ideally though the partners were well acquainted with one another's methods.

We now come to a more controversial subject, the arrangement of already existing music for ballet. One of the earliest and most famous examples is the Fokine-Chopin *Les Sylphides*, to many ballet lovers the most satisfying of all dance arrangements. The musical purist will immediately protest that the essence of this music is pianistic and that in any orchestrated version its percussive qualities are completely lost. Now I have a great respect for the musical purist—in his proper sphere, which is the concert hall and not the theatre. He is curiously hostile to theatre, in opera as well as ballet. We must remember that ballet is essentially an art of the theatre and must be judged by theatrical as well as musical standards. There must therefore in such cases be a compromise. We have to ask ourselves two questions : Is the resultant ballet good theatre ? Has so much violence been done to the form and spirit of the music that it upsets not only the musical purist but also the cultured theatregoer ? In the case of *Les Sylphides* let us admit that we are not listening to Chopin's music as it was composed but to something new, something which when it forms part of a ballet is remarkably effective. Ravel and Stravinsky, both of whom orchestrated *Les Sylphides*, undoubtedly took that point of view. Whether you can enjoy this orchestration in the cold atmosphere of the concert hall is another matter ; frankly I do not, except for reasons of association which are quite irrelevant to artistic judgment. The same can be said of Schumann's *Carnaval* and a number of other works. Constant Lambert has been conspicuously successful in his adaptations and arrangements of Auber, Meyerbeer and other composers, to whose works he has undoubtedly given a new spell of life.

In the case of the symphonic ballet we come upon another and very heated subject of controversy that in the palmy days when newsprint was abundant could compete in the Sunday papers as an item of interest with the latest trunk murder or society divorce. In 1933 and the following years Massine and de Basil launched the fashion with *Les Présages* to Tchaikovsky's Fifth Symphony, *Choreartium* to Brahms Fourth Symphony, *La Symphonie Fantastique* to Berlioz' symphony of that name. Later, for René Blum, Massine continued the series with Beethoven's Seventh Symphony. The musical purists immediately raised cries of "vandalism," "hands off the masters," "absolute music cannot be used for ballet." This term *absolute* or pure music, as some called it, requires explanation. Negatively it means music with no programme; positively it is less easy to define, because the term can only be used relatively. The dancer's claim is that any music that inspires in him a muscular reaction is fit for dancing, and the choreographer's justification is that although this music may be *absolute* to you it is not so to him. He can see in it a whole pattern of movement and sometimes even a theme that can be expressed dramatically. No one can deny that possibility, but the risk is very great. Everyone save the musical intellectual sees such images, but they may be so personal to the choreographer that he alone can feel and understand his interpretation. This risk is all the greater when very familiar music is used. Walt Disney tried it with Beethoven's Pastoral Symphony and personally I found the result disastrous much as I loved his flying horses for their own sake. His success in the same film with Tchaikovsky's *Casse Noisette*, even though the programme was his own, was undoubted. His purely abstract designs to a Bach fugue were interesting, but only in so far as they showed his personal reaction. In fact they intruded between the music and the average listener. Curiously enough

Massine found a staunch defender in the dean of musical critics, Ernest Newman. Newman wrote : "If music is to be ruled out from ballet when it is 'pure' music, what justification is there for *Les Sylphides* for example ? . . . We are bound to grant, I think, that there is nothing *a priori* incongruous in the making of 'pure' music, whether that of Brahms or of any other composer, with the lines and masses and movements of the ballet . . . the only question is to what extent the choreographer has succeeded." In his summing up he finds that Massine has done wonders.

Before dealing with his argument we must distinguish between the various symphonies used. No one could quarrel with the use of the *Symphonie Fantastique* which Berlioz wrote to a very definite programme. The choice of Tchaikovsky's Fifth Symphony can also be defended on the grounds that some contemporary critics found it too balletic in form. You have only to think of the third movement so brilliantly danced by Riabouchinska as Frivolity to realise that such music is thoroughly at home in the orchestra pit of a theatre. The real argument comes in the cases of Brahms and Beethoven. In *Choreartium*, his Brahms ballet, Massine has used no programme ; he has eliminated the dramatic partner and interpreted music by movement. To me the whole argument rests on whether this is good theatre or not and in that case it all boils down to a question of timing. The time element is the sole difference in the use of music between *Les Sylphides* and *Choreartium* ; that is the true answer to Newman. Brahms can develop and sustain a theme at a greater length than any dancer and so you have certain periods of *fade-out* on the stage. You had similar though far shorter periods in the de Valois-Bliss *Checkmate*, a commissioned ballet, purely because of this question of timing. Again, in the case of the Brahms Fourth Symphony certain passages lent themselves to the lifting of the dancers in the air in a fine architectural pattern, but there was nothing in the music to allow them to come to earth again. As they did not float through the ceiling there was a sharp contradiction between music and dance. Do you remember those *pirouettes* of the male dancers in the last movement? They would have illustrated the music very crudely I admit, if they could have been performed nightly with mechanical precision. They never were and the contradiction was painful. When you are dealing with such a master of pattern and movement as Massine it is impossible not to have many great moments in such a work where at times the parallelism between movement and music is extraordinarily happy; there were many really great moments of choreography, but the use of such music does not make for *complete* ballets and abstract dancing soon develops into a very dull formula, setting an almost insuperable problem for the decorative artist whose costumes and scenery must remind us of no period or country. Notice how closely interwoven are the arts that compose ballet. With Beethoven's Seventh Symphony the mistake came from the very conception of the work, the wedding of the music to a very definite theme, the creation of the world. Let us admit that Massine visualised this theme from the music; I—and one must speak personally—could not, so that the impression was jarring in the extreme. The fact that Wagner called this Symphony the apotheosis of the dance is not only no justification but a very positive condemnation of its use. Remember that Wagner said this before the music had been in any way allied to dancing.

It is very difficult indeed, quite apart from this question of timing, to lay down hard and fast rules as to the suitability of music for dancing. It is all a question of personal sensitivity and experience. There is quite clearly music that lends itself to direct narrative and music that is more reminiscent. A fine example is Rimsky-Korsakov's *Schéhérazade*, written to one programme but used for another. This is definitely music in the present tense, the music of action, of direct narrative. Balakireff's *Thamar*, far finer musically, which was used for the oriental successor to *Schéhérazade*, is much less direct. Constant

Lambert, a magnificent judge of such matters, gives us these examples.

There is another case, Nijinsky's *L'Après midi d'un Faune* to Debussy's music. Here there is no contradiction between the music and Mallarmé's poem ; the contradiction lies in the use Nijinsky has made of this music. His movement is jerky and angular while the music calls for a fluid and flowing line. Stravinsky in his memoirs stresses Nijinsky's musical ignorance.

These then are a few of the problems involved. Is it to be wondered at that choreographers are so very scarce ? That is one of our main problems in ballet. There is no lack of public demand or of reasonably skilled dancers but of people to make them dance. The choreographer needs a very special knowledge of music before he can apply it to the dance, and while the dancer's musical education can and certainly will be improved, it cannot go far enough to do anything but to serve her own needs as an individual.

Finally, let me ask you when next you visit the ballet, in spite of the fact that music is your special interest, not to judge it isolated from what you are seeing. You must look and listen and then judge the music as one of the four partners that compose ballet. Ballet stands or falls as a whole.

IV

BALLET AND DRAMA

Of all the arts dancing is the closest to us. We are said to dance with pain, anger or joy and while those are figures of speech they indicate how very much the dance is a part of ourselves. The dance serves magic and religion, primitive man in Central Australia and New Guinea, more sophisticated man in Java and Indo-China, neo-primitives in our dance halls.

The type of dancing that concerns us to-night is ballet, a Western European theatrical form, evolved at the court of a French king out of the dancing of the court, the peasant and the tumbler at the fair. Ballet dancing is but one part of the whole that is ballet, an art form compounded of dance, music, drama and the plastic arts. It is my aim to discuss and analyse the terms "theatrical dance" and the role played by drama in ballet. On its understanding in the first place depends the whole success or failure of a ballet irrespective of how good the dancing may be. It is a great pity that we are so restricted in the words we can use—ballet may mean either a technique of the dance, an art of the theatre or a company of dancers.

First let us be quite clear what it is that can be expressed concretely in this ballet medium. You cannot tell the audience about the past or of what may happen in the future. You are dealing with action in the present. "I love you now" and not "I used to love you once" or "I may grow to love you." That is, of course, an extreme simplification. Again, you cannot use ballet to convey precise and detailed information: "There is a £500 mortgage on the old homestead, if only we can hold out till the football pool results are in." It follows then that if in order to be intelligible a ballet requires a mass of written commentary in the programme, the producer has failed to use his medium correctly. Of course the understanding of audiences varies, also it grows with the ballet habit. I am talking now of that vague concept " the average cultured theatregoer " who is presumed to know the story of Cinderella and the four or five other fables upon which most ballet, and for that matter most drama and fiction are based.

If the medium of ballet is more limited than spoken drama in one direction, it is very much wider in another. Take *Petrouchka*, greatest of all dramatic ballets. Your ordinary unimaginative theatregoer will enjoy it as a brightly coloured nursery tale, the love-story of three puppets. Someone with more imagination will read into it the story of the awakening of a soul and, believe it or not, I once went to see it with an ardent communist who was convinced that it was a dramatic exposition of Karl Marx's theories. I couldn't see that myself, and I am quite sure that half the symbols that intense people read into a ballet are not intended by the choreographer. No matter ; the important thing is that a ballet can have as many different meanings as there are people watching it, ranging from the matter of fact to the highly imaginative.

Now for some of the laws governing the use of drama in ballet, basic laws that must be understood from the very first. Ballet must not have a purely literary inspiration. Year in and year out I receive a batch of long scenarios or sometimes just a post-card, saying : " Dear Sir, wouldn't Pickwick Papers make a wonderful ballet." I warn you that these efforts always find their way into the wastepaper basket where they belong. Inspiration must in the first place be musical or plastic. This needs some explanation, for you may argue that anything that is put into words is literary. For instance, that beautiful *pas de deux*, *Le Spectre de la Rose*, was suggested to a poet, Jean Louis Vandoyer, by a poem of Gautier's. Let us take three recent examples that provide a striking illustration of the use of drama in ballet.

Everyman is a miracle play of great and enduring beauty, something very complete in itself. Where then is the point in getting rid of most of the words and producing it as a ballet? Moreover, the producer is faced with a delicate problem—how to wed this truncated play to music. The solution he adopted was to borrow symphonic poems from Richard Strauss of all composers and written with a different programme in view—between ourselves I think that Johann Strauss would have been equally suitable. The net result to many is a spoilt play and spoilt music, both of which do not add up to good ballet, however carefully everything else has been done, and the work in question is magnificently dressed. Take the next example *Twelfth Night*, once again a play complete in itself. What happens in this case? You take a play by Shakespeare and then proceed to get rid of Shakespeare. You are now left with a very indifferent anecdote, which you or I, ladies and gentlemen, could have written any morning of the week between bath and breakfast. Once again you are faced with a musical problem. In this case the answer was Grieg, as it happens not altogether an inappropriate choice. It is clear that in both these cases the germ of the ballet did not come pictorially through an idea of movement, but through a process of faulty reasoning that said, "These are good plays, they should make equally good ballets." You will immediately think of another recent ballet, *Hamlet*, but this is an entirely different matter. Helpmann has not for a moment attempted to give us a wordless *Hamlet* and his ballet should really have been called "Perchance to Dream," for it is based on a purely plastic idea, the delirious dream that runs through Hamlet's imagination at the moment of death. Indeed it would be difficult to imagine such a vision being shown in any other medium.

When I warned you against the literary inspiration you can now see that I was too sweeping; the matter is not as simple as all that. Poetry and romantic literature often do contain the germ of an idea, but only if that idea is completely translated as in the case of Helpmann's *Hamlet* and Fokine's *Spectre de la Rose*. Ashton's *Quest*, for instance, based on an episode in Spenser's *Faerie Queene*, seems to me to suffer from incomplete translation;

too much positive story remains. It has not been used to set the imagination working.

At this point you may quite rightly feel like asking me, "Well, how is a ballet actually created ?" and though I have seen very many ballets in process of creation I cannot give you a clear answer. A musician, a painter and a dancer meet over the supper table and out of their talk a ballet is created. Often they themselves are unaware of what is happening. To this day there are disputes as to the origin of *Schéhérazade*, each party claiming the idea. *Petrouchka* came about through a piano melody that Stravinsky played, through Benois' interest in Russian fairs, because the ensuing talk inspired Fokine. That was Diaghileff's great role, to provide the meeting-place for artistes, to guide the conversation, to see that it had practical expression. One thing is certain, no ballet has originated through someone preparing a scenario of "War and Peace" or a play by Shakespeare and then hunting for an appropriate composer.

Once the subject has been selected the next important thing lies in its treatment. It must be realistic. That sounds like a contradiction of everything I have been saying. I mean, of course, realistic within the convention of ballet, where movement tells the whole story. We are still a little vague about this ballet convention because it is not yet as familiar as other artistic conventions. In the ordinary drama you do not feel embarrassed when you listen to the Joneses having a violent domestic quarrel. You are so accustomed to this theatre convention of no fourth wall that you don't give it a thought. It is the same thing in an art gallery. When you see a bronze bust of Alderman Binks you don't say, "Poor man what an odd colour ; he must be suffering from some skin disease." You are too familiar with that particular convention. All art has its rules and must be true to those rules. When in your ballet the scene is a fairy glade it would be unrealistic or implausible, if you prefer it, for those fairies to come bounding in in Russian boots. You smile, yet that is exactly what did happen, only in reverse, before the

Diaghileff-Fokine reforms. Whatever the place or the period, your dancers came tripping in on the tips of their toes smiling toothily. One of the reasons that for a long time ballet has found more favour as a medium with the modern composer and scenic artist than opera is on account of its regard for plausibility. If you go to the opera with a doctor friend to see one of those harrowing affairs in which the heroine, trilling lustily all the while, is dying of pulmonary tuberculosis, and your doctor turns to you and says, " This is ridiculous ; the whole clinical picture is wrong. Now, in my sanatorium . . ."—you would quite rightly vote him a dull ignoramus : but if he says to you, " I simply cannot believe in this ; that woman weighs thirteen stone and what's more no one could ever fall in love with her," he is fully justified. Opera just as ballet is a theatre art ; the acting is as important as the singing. The Russians understood that and Stanislavsky and Sanine did for opera what Fokine did for ballet.

Now let us take a look at it from the performer's point of view. There is no separate thing called mime which is superimposed on movement. It is often imagined that dancers pull a series of faces in the mirror to which they give labels, " hate," " fear," " envy," " joy," and that these are then brought out for use at the appropriate moment in the drama. There was, it is true, a sign language called mime used in the old classical ballet ; hand-on-heart-means-I-love-you and that sort of thing. The main point about classical ballet is the dancing and the dancer's line, but every now and then the choreographer feels that he must insert a chunk of mime to catch up with the story. Fokine has told us that mime only survives in revivals or in pastiche and that acting is a part of the dance itself directly inspired by the music. Just as in opera both *aria* and *recitative* are clearly recognised as singing, so in ballet there is your *aria* dancing, the variations and adagios, and your *recitative* dancing, so frequent to-day in the dance dramas of Helpmann and de Valois.

I have made a sharp distinction between classical and contemporary ballet with regard to their relationship to drama.

You may well ask me, " What about *Giselle* ? " There is mime, but also acting that is a part of the dance ; the story is of great importance, yet there can be no inspiration from the music. All of which I admit. *Giselle* is a freak, its very survival in spite of its mediocre music proves that. It survives just because its drama, which is direct and admirably suited to the medium, gives such a magnificent opportunity to the dancer who must show joy, sorrow, despair and madness in the first act and classical aloofness in the second. *Giselle* is a dance drama that in some way anticipates our contemporary ballet. Let us keep a sense of proportion though ; it is absurd to call it, as many have done, the *Hamlet* of ballet. It is a true product of romanticism, closely related to *La Dame au Camélias*, if we must find a dramatic comparison.

I have continually mentioned the word drama, and it needs some explanation to make it quite clear in the sense I intend. Drama in ballet does not always tell a positive story as in *The Rake's Progress, Miracle in the Gorbals* or *Giselle*. Sometimes it sets out to tell a story but the story doesn't matter as in *Swan Lake*, where the beauty of movement, line and pattern are alone important. At other times it merely suggests an atmosphere, romantic as in *Carnaval* or eerie as in *Cotillon*, a really great ballet though I defy anyone to tell me the story in words. However, even when there is no story to be told the dancer is concerned with acting. *Les Sylphides*, a *suite de danses* rather than a ballet, sets one of the most difficult problems in acting. Take the *prélude*, supreme test of the romantic dancer. It is technically within the grasp of every intermediate student, yet how rarely is it danced even tolerably, not on account of the steps but because of the style and the facial expression. This is ballet totally removed from literature in which the clue to expression can only come from the music. There is another case familiar to many of you, that of *Le Spectre de la Rose*. Why does the audience invariably applaud in the wrong place, when the male dancer makes his spectacular leap out of the window ? Because they are not aware that any dramatic problem is involved and are content to applaud virtuosity for its own sake. Yet the drama comes to its climax just after that leap, when the adolescent sleeper awakes, a woman, matured by her experience at the ball. The male dancer is the virtuoso, conjured up in the young girl's dream, the ballerina is the actress, the centre and *raison d'être* of the whole episode. This is a great drama that embodies the very essence of Fokine's genius, and it was Fokine who restored drama to ballet.

There are many other problems involved but these are some of the points that you should look out for if you wish to gain the maximum artistic experience from ballet and, more important still, if you wish to be a critical audience. Our ballet to-day is good enough to deserve such an audience. But never lose sight of one thing, *ballet is a visual art* that must please and interest the eye. Do not get lost in a number of theories about the social mission of ballet, the dance drama and the like. Such muddled thinking gave birth to that atrocity, the Central European Dance. I have talked of Drama and Ballet; to-morrow I may talk of Music and Ballet or Painting and Ballet. These are but aspects of something that combines all the arts and presents them to you on the stage.

V

BALLET AND THE SCENIC ARTIST

EVERY form of art has its snobs, those people with no real standards of value who assert an opinion because it happens to be the smart thing of the moment. In the 1920s for instance it was smart to call every production *amusing*, even if it were a tragedy in which the stage was littered with corpses. Ballet has always abounded in such fashion snobs who assess both dancers and notions of production for reasons quite irrespective of their merit. The snob thing immediately before the war was to turn to your neighbour at a ballet *première* and say, "This is all very well, the choreography is magnificent. What a ground pattern! But you should have seen it in practice costume and on the bare stage. Then it really was significant."

That had the very great advantage of impressing your neighbour that you were one of those privileged few who had been admitted to a rehearsal. It also showed that you were one of those who wanted to free the dance. Before the war tiresome people were always proclaiming loudly about freeing the dance; from drama, from scenery and costume and even from music. I imagine that all this knight-errantry must originally have been inspired by some disappointed choreographer.

Now you can perfectly well free the dance from music, painting and drama and return to the æsthetics of the jungle clearing but, if you do so, you will lose ballet which is essentially a composite art in which dancing is one of four partners.

Shortly before the war the experiment of freeing the dance from costume and scenery was tried at Covent Garden. It proved highly revealing. The ballet chosen was *Les Présages* to the music of Tchaikovsky's Fifth Symphony. It was an admirable test case. Many people disliked André Masson's designs and certainly the costumes were singularly uninspired. *Les Présages* was on that single occasion given in practice costume in front of a cyclorama. I say ballet, but in actual fact it wasn't a ballet at all, for only a fragment remained. Even so bold a dancer as Woizikovski totally failed to suggest the figure of Fate and the whole pattern of the movement was killed by the cold, bare background. A ballet could be devised for such a background ; that is another matter. This one was not ; it was devised as a whole by Massine and Masson with the sleeping but all-important partnership of Tchaikovsky. The experiment killed that particular piece of artistic cant.

Having clearly established the fact that costume and scenery exist in ballet as of right, let us first consider costume. It bears a close physical relationship to the dancer. It is, in fact, a part of her body while she is dancing. For that reason the history of costume has affected the whole history of dance technique. At the court of Louis XIV the dress was long and heavy, it touched the ground. As a result the dance could only give a pattern along the floor with the stress on the graceful carriage of the body, the movement of the arms and the set of the head. La Camargo shortened the dress by a few inches, revealing her ankles as you can see in Lancret's famous painting. The result was the discovery of the feet, the beginnings of the *danse en l'air*, elevation, the *batterie*. Camargo's rival Sallé tried to free the body still further by adopting the Greek tunic in the ballet *Pygmalion*. She was too many years ahead of her age and failed. Then about the time of the French revolution there came a complete transformation with Maillot's invention of theatrical tights. Attention became focused on the legs often at the expense of the rest of the body. The traditional ballerina *tutu* is in fact the rim of a top, accentuating the role of the legs. The *Sylphides* dress on the other hand, attributed to the French artist, Eugène Lami, is the costume of romance and not of virtuosity. Isadora Duncan came to St. Petersburg at a time when the *tutu* reigned supreme, when the Russian dancer had just learned the Italian trick of the thirty-two *fouettés* and when audiences counted aloud and then applauded in their enthusiasm. Some misguided folk still do. The *tutu* was worn whatever the style or period of the ballet. Duncan among her many innovations sought to leave the body free for movement and launched the vogue of the Greek tunic where Sallé had failed over two centuries before. This freedom meant that the whole body was the dancer's instrument and that the legs were no longer the focal-point. Later we shall see exactly where this has led us.

The physical relationship between costume and dancer gives us one negative rule : costume must be designed so as not to impede the particular dance for which it is intended. That may seem obvious, but it is very often infringed, particularly in the use of cumbersome head-dresses. Some of Bakst's beautiful *Sleeping Princess* designs were too cumbersome in execution.

Costume must conform to the style and period of the dance : that is a positive rule, but it needs a little amplification. It is not sufficient to take an accurate costume and transfer it to the stage. First it will generally transgress that negative rule of ours by being too cumbersome. Then ballet has a truth or a reality of its own and the costume must be translated to conform to it. Let me give you a striking example of this. The charming ballet *Children's Tales* calls for a horse in one of its scenes. A horse was brought into rehearsal and Diaghileff immediately said, " Take that thing away, it doesn't look like a horse at all." And it didn't, but a plywood horse knocked together by the stage carpenter looked admirable. That is clearly understandable ; a horse in a very restricted place behind footlights strikes a jarring note. It does not belong to this new world of fantasy. Take yet another example, from a legitimate play this time. *The Garden of Allah*, Robert Hichens' one-time popular exotic, has a sand-storm in it. The producers, aiming at realism, got hold of a quantity of sand and blew it across the stage. On the first night the audience too found themselves buried in sand, real sand that got into throats and noses, but it looked all wrong. Clever lighting would have produced twice the effect. It is the same with costume: style must be preserved but the truth of real life must be translated into the truth of the stage. You have a fine example of that in Sophie Fedorovitch's lovely designs for Ashton's *Nocturne*. Those are not the actual evening wear of Monsieur and Madame but they give the exact impression of the gay Paris of her period and they are light to dance in. Perhaps the most striking example that can be found of such translation in all three media is *The Three Cornered Hat*. The raw material consists of Spanish folk-music, Spanish folk-dancing and peasant costume. Da Falla translates the music, Massine the dancing and Pablo Picasso the costumes and setting; the result, one of the most complete of all ballets and something truly Spanish.

The costume designer must realise that ballet is a convention and he must always think in terms of that convention. He must be familiar with the music that is being used, with the type of movement that is intended and also with the grouping. An isolated costume of beauty is not enough, it may even mar the whole. His task is not merely to dress or decorate the dancers, as if he were embellishing something already complete in itself, but to aid in that completion. Let us take a very familiar ballet, *Carnaval*. Imagine it performed against curtains in practice clothes. Now think of Bakst's setting and costumes. Can you doubt the very positive role that he played? He was an equal partner. I have had the misfortune on two occasions to see that particular ballet redressed. It fell completely flat. In *L'Après midi d'un Faune* where Nijinski's angular choreography is in sharp contradiction to Debussy's flowing music, Bakst is clearly the senior partner. His costumes convey the whole style and intention of the work. But you can find endless examples for yourselves by imagining any familiar work without its scenery and costumes. Would *Les Sylphides*, still be romantic without its tarlatan? Watch it at rehearsal and you will soon be disillusioned. That does not lessen the role of the choreographer; he designed it for the stage and no one was less deceived by such cant than Fokine.

A word of warning here to would-be designers of costumes. It is extremely important to know something of practical dressmaking and of the reaction to light of various materials. It is not sufficient to remain isolated in your studio. It is true that many distinguished artists without previous stage experience have, when designing a ballet, produced what are really paintings in their own characteristic idiom. It takes a dressmaker of extraordinary skill and artistry to translate those paintings in reality. The resulting costumes are a collaboration. You will find that all the great names in ballet design—Benois, Bakst, Gontcharova, our own much regretted Rex Whistler—have given drawings that are minute in their detail, real blue prints for the dressmaker. They choose the material themselves, pinning a sample to the sketch. I notice in the many designs that unfortunately I continue to receive in bulk that, for instance, there is never any indication what a costume looks like at the back. That then is a practical workshop matter to be borne in mind quite apart from the many æsthetic questions we have already considered.

We now come to the question of scenery. Very much misunderstanding as to its proper function is caused by the use of the borrowed French word *décor*. Scenery is not a decoration or an embellishment but a part of the whole. Its history in ballet has been parallel to that of music. Just as in the degenerate days of ballet there were composers not of music but of "ballet-music," a type of merchandise ordered by the yard, so there were painters of *ballet-décors* who could not be called artists. Their scenery went on the stereotyped lines that we see to-day in those dull and vulgar spectacular reviews—it is quite clear that managers have learnt nothing from C. B. Cochran. There were realistic built-up sets that left nothing to the imagination.

Inevitably, there was a garden with a decorative fountain in the background. This was such a regular feature that the girls in the back row of the *corps de ballet* were called "the girls near the fountain." Diaghileff altered the whole position. His movement was started by artists for artists. It was the painter Alexandra Benois, his first artistic adviser, who originally drew his attention to the medium of ballet and to its great value in attaining one of their main objects, which was to introduce Russian art to Western Europe. A few years later Diaghileff was able to say, "Ballet is to the modern artist what the fresco was to the artist of the renaissance, a rapid method of creation and of making his work known."

Benois' first work, *Le Pavilion d'Armide*, marks the very beginning of the contemporary phase of ballet. Benois is an expert in period and has combined imagination and truth in all his works. The revolution became complete with the glowing passionate colour of Leon Bakst. After *Schéhérazade* any return to the stereotyped set became an impossibility. Poiret borrowed Bakst's palette for his fashion designs; the great stores followed suit with their window dressings. And therein lies a lesson and a warning, both of which Diagheleff understood as no one else. When asked years later to revive *Schéhérazade* he said, "I would have to do so in a higher key not to fail; memory and imitations have painted the colours too bright and the public would be disappointed." In spite of every inducement he would never revive this epoch-making work. The sensational artistic development of the moment inevitably finds its way from stage and studio to the covers of *Vogue* and *Harper's Bazaar*, to the dressmakers, to the manufacturers of perfume and eventually to Woolworths. Surrealism has long lost its power to shock, tamed by the ingenious commercial artist and by Dali himself, who was one of the first to see its vast commercial possibilities. Just as Picasso has refused to conform to any formula, Diaghileff would never push a success to its limits. He tired of his creations while his public still demanded more in the same manner. The imaginative reconstructions of Benois, the exotic splendour of Bakst gave way to the grotesque of yet another Russian artist, Larionov, who, with Gontcharova, introduced the naïve quality of the Russian peasant. Massine's first ballet, *The Midnight Sun*, marks a new decorative phase, Diaghileff's second. The designer turns his back completely on any form of realism. If the scene calls for a chair, as long as it is not to be used for being sat on, he paints it on the backcloth ; not a chair to deceive but something that he depicts as the very essence of all chairs. Sunlight is not shown by the arcs ; the very source of light is painted as the big red blob of the peasant's imagination or the child's painting-book. We are living in a new world in which anything can happen. The artist's skill lies in making us believe in it. Walt Disney has carried this to its logical conclusion. In its extreme form it was always more suited to the puppet or animated drawing than to the human dancer who often found it difficult to make us believe that she belonged in such a world. Far happier has been *décor* that departs entirely from depicting natural objects and that is as abstract as the music. Miro's brilliant *Jeux d'enfants* built a completely new world in which Massine's creations convinced us of their reality.

The Russian Revolution cut Diaghileff off from the artists of his motherland and Paris became more and more his centre of inspiration for scenery and music. Picasso's *Parade* marks another decorative phase. Cubism was the talk of the day and *Parade* was more of a cubist manifesto than a successful ballet. When the decorative artist becomes the dominant partner I am always reminded of a quotation from *Nicholas Nickleby*. Vincent Crummles is talking to Nicholas :

> "We'll have a new show-piece out directly. . . . Let me see—peculiar resources of this establishment—new and splendid scenery—you must manage to introduce a real pump and two washing tubs."

" Into the piece ? " said Nicholas.

" Yes," replied the manager. " I bought 'em cheap, at a sale the other day and they'll come in admirably. That's the London plan. They look up some dresses, and properties, and have a piece written to fit 'em. Most of the theatres keep an author on purpose."

" Indeed ! " cried Nicholas.

" Oh yes," said the manager ; " a common thing. It'll look very well in the bills in separate lines : Real pump !—Splendid tubs !—Great attraction ! . . ."

In other words, instead of real pumps and splendid tubs, the artist has cubism, dadaism or surrealism in his studio, so the ballet must be written around them. Daighileff was too wise to allow himself to be habitually used to launch a studio fashion and the Paris School gave him such outstanding works as Picasso's *Three Cornered Hat*, Derain's *La Boutique Fantasque* and Laurencin's *Les Biches*. The Swedish Ballet of Rolf de Maré, however, was swamped by the brilliance of its own *décors* ; it became a Paris Studio plaything.

The essence of Diaghileff's work was the parallelism between the arts composing ballet. Each will struggle for supremacy; his role —and we still have no name for it—was to maintain the balance.

Post-Diaghileff Russian Ballet showed us nothing new scenically. The dancer had once again become the centre of attraction and it is significant in that connection that London and not Paris was de Basil's G.H.Q. De Basil was in a sense living on an overdraft from the previous régime. Some of his *décor* was of very great beauty, notably Bérard's *Symphonie Fantastique* and *Cotillon* and Miro's *Jeux d'enfants*, already mentioned, but the halt between tours was too brief for any settled plan. A *décor* just happened, and in the case of *La Symphonie Fantastique* Bérard was obviously familiar with music and programme and could work untroubled by the fact that the company was 4000 miles away.

One of the de Basil *décors* provides an interesting lesson. *Les Sylphides* was danced against an enlargement of a woodland painting by Corot. It seemed the obvious home for sylphs since Corot peopled his glades in this way, yet nothing could have been more unsuitable. This painting was complete on its own and as such attracted too much attention to itself. There is a parallel with music here. What is called absolute music is unsuited to ballet; this was an absolute picture. Time and care rather than such bright fancies are essential.

This time factor is all important. A company needs a permanent home in which to plan. Diaghileff had such a home in Monte Carlo. The leading artists of Europe were his guests there for many months in the year, meeting dancers and composers at every meal, watching class and rehearsals, always tactfully guided by Diaghileff himself. It is in that way that he was fully creative. When writing his biography I questioned the majority of his collaborators. "Diaghileff neither painted, danced, nor composed. How did he create?" "He didn't," the majority replied. "We did, he merely made the way easy." It is sufficient to say that, quite apart from what I myself witnessed on numerous occasions in London, Paris and Monte Carlo, not one of his collaborators ever achieved the same artistic success when they created away from him. Of course he was fully creative; his medium being ballet, that most neglected thing, *ballet as a whole*. When de Basil gave up Monte Carlo the decadence of Russian emigré ballet began.

Our own national ballet, Sadler's Wells, has gone through no distinctive decorative phases but has lately shown much work of real distinction. I would remind you of Rex Whistler's *Rake's Progress* and *Wise Virgins*, Messel's *Comus*, Furse's *Prospect Before Us*, Ayrton's *Festin de l'Araignée*, Chappell's *Patineurs* and *Les Rendezvous*, Fedorovitch's *Nocturne* and *Dante Sonata*, Hugh Stevenson's *Promenade*, Burra's *Miracle in the Gorbals*, Lord Berner's *Wedding Bouquet*, Chiang Yee's *The Birds*. Both Graham Sutherland and John Piper have dressed ballets but I feel that their collaboration was not quite complete, their visions not fully translated in the sense that I have explained.

The greatest discovery has been that of Leslie Hurry, a true discovery in the Diaghileff sense of the word. His *Hamlet* set was a part of the movement of that ballet of delirium and combined the romanticism of Tchaikovsky's music and the modernism of Helpmann's idea. In his *Swan Lake*—and his task with such a well-known work was a formidable one—he brought back the sparkle and the glamour to what in Western Europe has usually been a singularly drab, pre-Diaghileff setting, a mere background for dancers. Notice the extraordinary detail in his work, yet when properly lit it never creates a finicky effect but makes an immediate impression that steadily grows on one. Hurry is a true theatre artist. Both he and Edward Burra plunge us straight into the atmosphere of the ballet.

Just a word here on the use of drop scenes during an overture or musical interlude. They can be extraordinarily effective dramatically. Rex Whistler's fine architectural scene establishes the London of Hogarth, Berner's gives a foretaste of the deliberately naïve quality of his *Wedding Bouquet*, Burra indicates the squalor and the mystery of the Helpmann-Bentall *Gorbals*. In the *Prospect Before Us* Furse uses his painting for an entirely new and different purpose, to advance the narrative by showing the fire in the theatre. Such drop scenes are not used sufficiently. They have an important role to play in the creation of illusion.

So far we have dealt with the direct contribution that painting makes to ballet. There is another and more complex relationship, the debt that the choreographer owes to the painter. Museums are a rich source of choreographic inspiration. Let us take a few random examples. Massine's *Good Humoured Ladies* revealed a familiarity with Longhi, Nijinsky's *L'Après midi d'un Faune* with the sculpture of Attic Greece. But generally the inspiration is less obvious. It is something personal to the choreographer that has set a train of thought in motion. Diaghileff would always take his choreographers round the galleries for this very purpose. Sometimes the inspiration is far more direct. One of Ashton's juvenilia was a charming little work, *Florentine Picture*. The result of his museum studies came to full fruition in *The Wise Virgins*. De Valois has found direct inspiration from Blake in her masterly *Job* and from the narrative pictures of Hogarth in *The Rake's Progress* and Rowlandson in *The Prospect Before Us*. This is a particularly British departure just as the conversation piece and the narrative picture are essentially British.

Let us see exactly what this involves. The picture gives a static scene, one possible group in a long ballet. Merely to reproduce that scene is to give a *tableau vivant*, a direct contradiction of ballet which expresses itself in movement. The choreographer of such a work has to assimilate the style of the painter so thoroughly that he must depict a thousand possible paintings from the same hand. Also he must select the right painter. An impressionist, for example, interested in the effect of light on colour is not suitable, as we saw in the case of Manet's *Bar au Folies-Bergère*. I doubt whether the much used, or shall we say in this case abused, Degas is suitable for anything but a series of *tableaux vivants*. He is already dealing with the dancer in his own manner. In any case it is altogether a mistake to think of him as the painter of dancers. They served him as models just as his washerwomen and jockeys, and his particular vision does not lend itself well to stage translation. One of my objections—and I have many—to this alleged Greek dancing is that it is based, technique and all, on the static poses from vase paintings and sculpture. We have seen that such static poses can suggest a train of thought but they cannot logically be used to innovate a whole new technique of dancing. *L'Après midi d'un Faune* was a clever trick that exploited the artist's approach to the frieze, suggesting bas-relief. Neither that nor Fokine's *Daphnis and Chloe* were attempts at anything but a single ballet. Duncan danced supremely well because she was an inspired individual but her Grecian research was superficial and unimportant. Such artistic "sports" dance first and only then, usually when their power is waning, do they theorise.

You must be very well grounded in the orthodox technique to allow yourself the luxury of pictorial inspiration, otherwise you become nothing but a very indifferent copyist.

The enormous and deserved success of Sadler's Wells gives our contemporary British artists the opportunity of making their work known through Europe, and it has never been more important than now for us as the home audience to understand the painter's role in ballet; a role that is far less obvious than that of the other partners. The next time that you visit the ballet think of these things. There are many important points that you will be able to add to this necessarily bare outline. But whatever you do, don't say, "The ballet was splendid but the scenery and costumes bad," or the reverse. Only by judging what you see as a whole will you show that true understanding so essential at the present day.

VI

BALLET AND THE CHOREOGRAPHER

You will find in your ballet programmes a difficult and unpleasant sounding word " choreography " or " choreographer." It may well be Greek to you. It is in fact derived from the Greek ; *Xoros*, a dance and *grapho*, to write. The little *Oxford Dictionary* defines it as " designer of ballet."

The word is unusual and difficult ; the function that it describes is equally unusual and difficult. There is no school of choreography, no choreographic manual, no practical method of recording choreography. What an appalling number of negatives ! Let us build up a few positives.

The dictionary is not altogether accurate in its definition. No single person to-day designs ballet. *The choreographer is the designer of that portion of ballet that is danced ;* a very different matter, since ballet also requires a composer, a painter and at times a poet. I find that many people visiting ballet for the first time imagine that the dancers are inventing the steps as they go along. These people ask, " Is it always the same every performance ? " They find it difficult to imagine that choreography is as positive and unvaried—or shall I say, should be—as a script or score. In a recent copyright case both the learned judge and counsel believed that ballet was an improvisation, and indulged in some heavy judicial wit before they were disabused.

I am going to take our choreographer from the start of his career and try and explain upon what it is that he builds his craft and possibly his art.

The choreographer is invariably a dancer, trained for years in the classical technique of ballet. That technique gives him a very large vocabulary of steps that can be combined in sentences or what are called *enchainements*. If he works purely with his classroom vocabulary, the result will be a schoolpiece in which his dancers can show their paces, but it will lack originality or any trace of personality. His very urge to create is generally brought about through a natural reaction from the classicism that he practises daily. His first tentative experiment will be with his own body and in some role that he fancies himself. Nearly every young choreographer is his own leading dancer. At the same time, being a member of a company he knows the capabilities and limitations of his colleagues. His début is probably a very subjective affair.

So far I have made it seem comparatively simple. I have talked of the choreographer's reaction to his own art of dancing. His greatest problem is the use that he is going to make of music. The choreographer must be musical and he must be musical in a practical manner, very much in the manner of a conductor. If he is using typical ballet music, then he is only concerned with counting, but the contemporary ballet score is a much more complicated affair. Make a mental comparison between *Giselle* and, say, *Petrouchka* and you will realise how complex it has all become. The choreographer is, in fact, concerned with the orchestration of dancers, with human counterpoint. The first choreographers were all musicians ; only later did the division of functions take place, when dancing became a highly specialised art. But this early combination of the two functions does show the extent to which the choreographer must be a musician.

Our choreographer has now been confronted by two of the arts that are his concern, dancing and music. If he is content to give us a classical pastiche, he is amply equipped. But in most cases the music calls for interpretation in narrative form which he and the composer or some third party may have sketched out. He is now concerned with the art of drama ; he must create characters and with them tell his story in direct narrative easily understood by his audience. There are various ways in which he can create his characters, by making them act with their faces, by regulating their movements so that the dance itself suggests an individual, or by combining the two. The *ballet d'action*, or narrative ballet, is composed of two types of dancing: "the set piece or *aria*," such as an *adagio* which is a duologue, usually a love duet, a variation which is a monologue, a *pas de quatre* or the dance of a whole *corps de ballet*; and the other type which we might call *recitative dancing*, in which the story is developed. Let me take an example from Frederick Ashton's *Nocturne*, a very perfect ballet by a master choreographer. The Flower Girl's dance is a monologue in which she indicates her state, despair and loneliness. The passage where the watcher, through whose eyes we see the story, moves for the first time to approach the prostrate girl and comforts her and then walks to the balustrade to greet the rising sun is *recitative*. It tells the last chapter of the drama. It is important to recognise that it is dancing, that it depends on the music and is not a bit of acting superimposed upon the ballet. This creation of character in ballet is a delicate business that varies from a flat type such as Dr. Coppelius, in which heavy make-up plays its part, to the fey child so brilliantly danced by Riabouchinska in *Jeux d'enfants*, from the stock characters of the *Comedia dell' Arte* to the suicide in the Gorbals. This young girl is brilliantly revealed in her dance at rebirth; she is shown us in the "round." Ninette de Valois in *Checkmate* makes superb use of characterisation. This is a balletic game of chess but by enlisting our sympathy for the Red King and his consort she makes the struggle dramatically exciting. We take sides. Contemporary English ballet is developing this, the dance drama aspect of choreography. De Valois and Helpmann in England and Antony Tudor in America have all made important contributions in that direction. It can be exceedingly dangerous if not handled by choreographers who have learnt a respect for the classical dance. It can degenerate into the wordless play in which the audience's reaction will be, "for God's sake speak."

Quite apart from the combination of movement, music and drama the choreographer is concerned with a pattern that must be pleasing in itself. That is the essence of classicism. Classical ballet has a story, the story matters very little. What is important is beauty of line and fluidity of movement. Take the *arabesque*, for instance. The line of the body with its long curve is important in itself and complete in itself apart from any dramatic context. The *attitude* is a magnificent piece of sculpture, while the easy-flowing transition from step to step apart from any meaning that can be expressed in words, represents dancing at its finest. There is a close parallel between classicism in painting and in ballet. The story of a painting by Ingres is ignored, his line is all important. To adapt his famous adage : " La danse c'est la probité de l'art."

As long as the designers of a dance-drama bear all this in mind there is no danger. Helpmann's lovers in *The Miracle in the Gorbals*, de Valois' Red Queen in *Checkmate* or her pathetic young girl in *The Rake's Progress* are beautiful in themselves as well as being part of a quickly moving narrative. Frederick Ashton is in the great European tradition of Fokine and Balanchine. His narrative is always subservient to beauty of movement for its own sake ; the accent is on dance rather than drama. It is largely a question of temperament which type of ballet one prefers, but undoubtedly after the first shock of a new ballet-drama the interest veers more and more towards the actual dancing itself. Taken from that point of view de Valois' *Promenade*, a dancer's ballet, seems to me an addition to the repertoire that will long endure. I cannot agree with those critics who claim that pure dancing is limited and monotonous. It is only so when badly used or executed and in that case the dance-drama too would easily lend itself to ridicule. We can see the great difficulties of choreography and the extraordinary balance required and there can be little wonder at the fact that choreographers are and always have been scarce. In his quarter century Diaghileff only used five. Choreography is not an independent art, the choreographer is never a free agent to express himself completely.

Hitherto the problems I have mentioned are æsthetic. There are practical problems as well.

Always remember that in the theatre a ballet company alone has to create its own works. It cannot, like the dramatic or operatic companies, find its next work on the library shelf. This means that the choreographer cannot begin to rehearse a ballet *with* the company before having composed a ballet *on* that company. He demands from his artistes greater time, effort and concentration than any other producer. He must be able to inspire loyalty and a strong belief in himself. I have seen many with really interesting ideas fail in that respect so that those ideas have never become concrete. He must be a pedagogue with all the knowledge of psychology that is involved.

We now come to the interesting and often asked question, how far do the dancers collaborate in the actual creation of a ballet? The answer must vary considerably; with the strong choreographer very little, assuming that he has a capable company, though even a Fokine will have his scope of expression enormously expanded by having such a ballerina as Karsavina. Massine in his de Basil phase was able to introduce many innovations in movement through the extraordinary virtuosity of Baronova, and Toumanova and Balanchine undoubtedly made capital of their immaturity, with the result that many of his works date and suffer damage with changes of cast.

It was Michael Fokine who gave us the whole æsthetic of our contemporary ballet and to me he remains the outstanding choreographer. As a dancer he was trained in the finest school in the world. He passed through dramatic academy. He was a painter of considerable technical merit. He could read an orchestral score with the ease of a conductor. He was a strict disciplinarian with the ability of conveying exactly what he wanted his company to do. I watched him at work over a number of years. He explained the exact meaning of his plot and the style involved. He was able to act every role so that his meaning was magnificently clear. And everywhere he went he kept his eyes open. He would watch the movements of a *maître d'hotel* and afterwards mimic them to perfection, or look at the children playing in the street, storing up every gesture for future use. It is difficult for us at the present day when we mistakenly call his *Sylphides* a classic—and so it is, but in the secondary sense of that word—to realise the fierce opposition that his work raised. Without it ballet would be a dying art. He was a great evolutionary and not a revolutionary ; he did not destroy the technique that had nurtured him, he adapted it. Let us take a look at some of his work and compare it to the surviving classics, always remembering that they are the sole survivors of many hundreds and therefore works of rare merit among what must have been a mediocre average. The Blue Bird from *The Sleeping Princess* is a virtuoso dance of extraordinary beauty ; *The Dying Swan* is a moving drama based on a simple *pas de bourrée* ; the final *adagio* in *Casse-Noisette* is a difficult technical feat ; the *pas de deux* in *Le Spectre de la Rose*, technically simple, artistically difficult, is part of a delicate study in adolescence ; *Giselle* is a romantic drama, or rather a melodrama, that undoubtedly has elements of true greatness or it would never have survived ; *Les Sylphides* has captured the very essence of romanticism with none of the claptrap. Do not think for a moment that I am condemning classicism. I am merely trying to show that without destroying anything in the dance Fokine gave us ballet as a whole. With him the story does not yet intrude, the pleasure is still as visual as with the classics, and the visual element is always the first essential. It is well to remember this, for it is of the nature of ballet that with his death his works with all their fine detail will gradually disappear.

Nijinsky, his immediate successor in the Diaghileff ballet, accomplished but little. He was ill equipped musically for choreography and *L'Apres midi d'un Faune*, which survives, owes its interest largely to Bakst.

Our next choreographer, Leonide Massine, is a very great figure who has enormously enriched the repertoire of movement in ballet, borrowing from folk-dancing and the primitive dance and adapting the result to ballet. He is infinitely versatile, with a great and restless intelligence to which are due both his virtues and his faults. His *Good Humoured Ladies, Three Cornered Hat, La Boutique Fantasque, Jeux d'enfants, Beau Danube, Les Présages, Symphonie Fantastique* and certain passages in *Choreartium* show the extraordinary scope of his work. I see that his recent work in America has displeased the critics, who now dismiss him as a back number. It may be that he has struck a bad patch and that he finds conditions in America unsuited to creation ; he is essentially a European who needs the inspiration of Paris. But I should be very surprised if he were in fact a back number. Many years ago he struck a similar bad patch in America, where Fokine also was unable to create, but on his return to Europe we saw some of his finest work. Personally, and through a long experience of Massine, I should be surprised to find even his failures—and I regard *Gaieté Parisienne* as one of them—totally devoid of stimulating passages. The restless commercial atmosphere of large travelling companies is inimical to creation. Massine is a master who cannot be judged by the dictates of passing fashion. I have seen his *Boutique Fantasque* lightly dismissed in an article by a reputable critic who used it to laud Antony Tudor's very charming *Jardin au lilas* to the skies. I can only marvel at such a lack of standards.

Balanchine stands high as a choreographer of great musicianship and subtlety ; indeed, over-subtlety may be his fault. The greatest of his works that we have seen in this country is *Cotillon*, that extraordinary incursion into the dream-world. Balanchine is essentially an artist's artist whose work can best be appreciated by the choreographer and musician. In his use of the classical idiom he is nearer to Fokine than any other choreographer, but whereas Fokine was a romantic Balanchine is interested in movement for its own sake. Unfortunately all that we have seen of his recent work has been on the films. It has been as good or as bad as all such work.

The manner in which you assess choreographers will always depend on your attitude to ballet in general, whether you are a classicist, a romantic or a realist. But in any case let me repeat that whether the ballet is a dance-drama or a display of pure dancing the all-important thing is the visual effect and the relationship between each successive movement. Movement is important in itself and should be significant and beautiful apart from the programme. I have already mentioned our English choreographers, about whom I have written extensively during the last few years. Our company is unique in one particular, in having three choreographers working together in close harmony, each one with a highly individual style. In *Job*, *Dante Sonata* and *The Miracle in the Gorbals*, or *The Rake's Progress*, *Nocturne* and *Hamlet*, we have examples of every type of choreographic thought.

Fashion alters in choreography as in painting or music, from classicism to romanticism or realism. But its basic principles are unchanging. A Noverre writes for all time. As an audience the safeguarding of those principles lies in your hands. Modern ballet requires people of understanding and not "fans." The "fan" would soon destroy what has been built up with such great skill and understanding by a Fokine or a de Valois. Don't applaud by habit, because it is the polite thing to do. That has often been a weakness of British audiences who are notoriously kind-hearted. Applause must only be the reward for work well done. We want not merely entertainment but an art that has evolved and is still evolving out a of great tradition.

VII

BALLET CLUBS : THEIR RUNNING AND THEIR FUNCTION

THIS is the inaugural meeting of your ballet club and I am delighted to be present because it gives me the opportunity of saying many of those things that I have felt very strongly through my experience of such clubs. I am going to be very frank because I believe that only by so doing can I be useful to you.

Of course you are aiming at a production and as that is the ambition uppermost in all your minds I will start there, although *you* most decidedly should not.

Without fancying myself as a prophet I will put it on record that with your very first show you will undoubtedly have a major success. Please don't let that cheer you up. How could you possibly avoid a triumph ? You will have in one capacity or another some fifty persons involved in your production, each one of whom has loving relations and friends who can be counted upon to fill the hall and to make the appropriate noises of approval. Then you will find your press extraordinarily kind. " Miss Smith is dainty, Miss Brown a marvel of Terpsichorean grace," all of which will show, to those who are used to reading such notices, that they are not taking you very seriously. I beg you to discount all such success in advance. Pass a resolution to that effect this very night and enter it in your minutes. It is painfully easy to be taken in by it and so to lose all your standards. In any case your troubles are far from over, because with this certain success you are bound to have serious disagreements within your committee about the distribution of roles and credit. It has happened in the X, the Y and the Z ballet clubs.

No, I am not a cynic. On the contrary, I am an enthusiast

who strongly believes in the value of what you are setting out to do ; but I am also a practical man with a very large experience of such matters and I want to warn you of the many difficulties you will meet, those that can be avoided by a little cool and critical thinking.

Let us start at the very beginning ; we shall return to your production in due course. You begin with a committee and a set of rules. There can be no doubt that this club was called into being by the dancing and ballet-loving members of the community. Remember that ballet is a composite art and that not only dancers but musicians and painters must have equal representation on your committee. You cannot possibly create without them. Start by forming some link with the music and art students in your city. Invite their professors to become honorary members. If they have the time and inclination, they are the very people for your committee and you are already half-way to real success.

Make your bye-laws elastic. You will find that they need altering as you go along, and many young societies are strangled by rigid rules from the very first meeting. You will need officers to look after the treasury, the secretariat and the educational programme as well as a production committee with a musical, an arts and a choreographic director. The smaller your working committee the better, though there are many vitally important subsidiary roles such as the provider of buns and tea at meetings and rehearsals and her deputy. One of my favourite clubs has harnessed its mothers for this and equally arduous tasks. All is peace.

The first and easiest thing to fix is an educational programme which should consist of lectures on all the arts, discussion groups, gramophone recitals and so on. The very fact of artists in so many media meeting together is important. Such interchanges of artistic opinion have always been lacking in England where the painter knows nothing of the musician and the novelist is not sufficiently conversant with painting to choose his own dustcover. In France there is scarcely an author of repute who has not written a volume or two of art criticism. But then France has the café, glorious meeting-place of the muses. Your club must serve as a substitute. I see that Manchester in their very complete programme has week-end rambles, an admirable item that has a direct bearing on the object you have in view, that of mixing together and understanding one another. The art members can use the dancing members as models in a sketching meeting, dancers can demonstrate *cnchainements* to the musicians, and so on.

Now for this question of a production. First wait until your club has achieved some harmony and take a very long time with your planning. You can afford that luxury. You must realise that your performance can be marred from the very first on paper or, perhaps I should say, because it has not been worked out on paper. The first thing to mark on that agenda is the time at your disposal. Make your performance as short as possible, from sixty to eighty minutes of actual dancing ; that means three or four fifteen-minute, ballets and a *divertissement*. No unpractised choreographer can possibly hold the interest of an audience for more than fifteen minutes, especially when using unpractised dancers. I find people have an extraordinary idea about the time that ballets last unless they have had to use a stop-watch. A dance of one minute and a half can seem endless ; in that time a dancer can express a very great deal.

Now for the ballets themselves. First for a bit of negative advice. Do not aim at originality or what is usually wrongly called modernism, which you cannot possibly handle. If you are an original thinker, it will emerge whatever you do. Some people are so terrified of being pretty that they plunge headlong into ugliness under the mistaken impression that they are showing character. Next, you must take careful stock of the dancing material available. What are you dancers' technical resources ? Have you a ballet club ballerina ? Aim at some simple poetical idea, use music that is suitable, that can be played effectively on your pianos or small orchestra, and that you have not had to disfigure by cuts and repeats. Take musical advice ; I am never tired of repeating it. Use the classical technique, those enchainments that you know ; from them endless combinations can be devised. Finally with costumes ; remember, designers, that your drawing is a blue print from which the costumes will be made. Only the designer who knows that a great costumier is working with him can afford the luxury of a slapdash drawing ; which in fact means that the costumier is doing half the work. As in the case of your dancers, always think in terms of material available in the shops and of your budget. If you use scenery, remember the shape of the hall or theatre in which the performance is to take place. I have seen a good ballet ruined for lack of such a precaution. Similarly you must rehearse at least twice on the actual stage. Now the one person who must be experienced is the stage manager who controls your lighting, is in charge of timing and so on. Hire a professional stage manager. You will not regret it.

You will probably need a *divertissement* to give all your talent a chance. In professional ballet a *divertissement* is somewhat suspect ; Pavlova, as always, being the magnificent exception. Your aim is to give opportunities to as many as possible, dancers as well as choreographers. Remember here to keep your dances short—I repeat, a great deal can be expressed in one minute. Try also not to make this *divertissement* too violent a musical mixture. If you are putting on national dances, correctness of style and costume are most important. Finally, if I hear that anyone has dared to dance *The Dying Swan*, I will turn up at the dress rehearsal with a tommy-gun. No jury of taste and discrimination would dare to convict. I must take my chance.

A programme needs balance. A great deal of time is spent in the great professional companies in securing such balance. Certain ballets, for instance, always open the evening, *Les Sylphides*, *Carnaval*, *Les Rendezvous* ; while others form a perfect ending, *Prince Igor*, *Le Beau Danube*, *Façade*. You must lead your audience gently into this world of illusion with a romantic one, place your more thoughtful work in the middle and send them home thrilled or amused. Each ballet has a personality; their sum total, the programme, has a personality of its own. At first there is no way of knowing what your members have to offer. Audition meetings for group works or *solistes* are of great value; and also what I might call "lightning sketch" evenings in which your members listen to an air and then improvise a dance. That is very excellent training for the dancer as well as the musician. Don't forget, you musician members, that you are not just accompanists. Hold out against distorting the tempo so that the dancers can make certain effects. They will most certainly try to persuade you. On the other hand, remember that you are in the theatre and not the concert hall and that some compromise is necessary. No one understands the relationship between music and the dance better than Constant Lambert. Study his arrangements; they are masterly and have given our national ballet its present-day status.

You may feel that I have gone out of my way to underline difficulties and to discourage you from adopting a bold policy of discovery. That is not the case. You have a very real and important role to play in the ballet world. Your function is that of the laboratory or, since that suggests those ungraceful animals, guinea-pigs, let me say dance studio. There exists no school of choreography, the ballet club can take its place. Dramatic societies are not expected to produce playwrights, but your activities must be fully creative. If you need help, advice or really frank criticism, I know that the Production Club, a protégé of the Royal Academy of Dancing, will be only too pleased to send a competent representative to your performance. We are most interested in all you have to show and wish you every possible success, for your triumph will be a triumph for the art we love and are trying to serve.

Q. If there is to be a Scottish national ballet, use must be made of Highland dancing which lends itself to ballet. Do you agree?

A. I was expecting that question as my nationalist friend has already raised it at previous lectures last year. I am pleased it has come up again, because there are two basic principles involved.

No ballet company can set out deliberately to be national with any hope of success. Before the war the Polish Ballet was founded on that principle and naturally failed through lack of variety. Nijinska, a Russianised Pole with an international outlook, warned them but it was in vain. The Russian Ballet was a Russian Ballet but with no insistence on creating works in the national idiom. In due course a *Petrouchka* happened. Our Sadler's Wells operates in the same way. It has created a *Rake's Progress.* Had de Valois sat down and concentrated on how British she could be there would be no Sadler's Wells, Britain's national ballet at the present moment. Your preoccupation with tartans would kill a Scottish company if it ever got started; and I very much hope it will.

I agree with you that the dance material is extraordinarily rich and that it bears a close relationship to ballet which, in common with basque and other folk-dancing, it has influenced. It will most certainly be used one day but it requires a great deal of digesting. It is not designed for the theatre at all in the first place but for the open air. You cannot take it intact and just dump it on to the stage. It needs careful translation into its new medium; a true expert's job. The supreme example of such translation is the da Falla-Picasso-Massine *Three Cornered Hat* in which folk-music, costume and dance of Spain were made into a very great ballet. This ballet was danced by a Russian cast, headed by

Karsavina and Massine, and it delighted Spanish audiences who are intensely proud of their national dance. There is a lesson in that. Your dance, your ballads, your music and costume all await such translation.

Q. I am a strong upholder of the Cecchetti method. What do you think of it?

A. That is altogether outside my province, but it does give me the opportunity of saying something that may be of help. I often watched Cecchetti's class and greatly admired his great gifts as a teacher. There is no magic virtue in a system as such and I am quite sure that neither Cecchetti nor any other great master thought for one moment in terms of systems. Obviously a system is necessary but strict adherence to it will not make a dull teacher inspiring. The perfect teacher knows that you cannot fit all individuals into a rigid system. That is the essence of fine teaching, the realisation that differences of temperament and of physique require a different approach. One cannot sit down at a table and discuss Cecchetti and Royal Academy work in the abstract; the great thing is who is to teach them and how are they to be taught. Sometimes a combination of methods gives brilliant results. The great Russian ballerinas were pupils of Johannsen as well as Cecchetti. Shortcomings in teaching have little to do with a syllabus; they come from a lack of knowledge of pedagogy. Your historian may have his head crammed with knowledge and yet be completely ineffective in the lecture hall. The average teacher needs a training college to learn the psychology of teaching. The Royal Academy of Dancing has such a course. The brilliant teachers such as Preobrajenska will never follow any one method blindly.

Please do not think that I am decrying the need or the value of a definite syllabus. This is a plea for the right way of using and understanding it, for not worshipping it blindly as an idol. Medicine similarly misunderstood leads to the wearing of a prescription round the neck as an amulet.

Q. Where would you place Jooss in your scheme of things?

A. I wonder where Jooss places himself? Strictly speaking he does not belong in a lecture on ballet because he does not practise or approve of ballet technique except in a modified form. However, I am not going to avoid your question, because I greatly admire Jooss and believe that he has a great deal to offer us.

There are two extremes in ballet; dancing for the sake of dancing, for the resultant beauty of line and movement; and the telling of a story with great economy of movement, where the main accent is on the message to be projected across the footlights. Those are, as I have said, extremes, and there are endless gradations in between. Classical ballet tends towards the first extreme and contemporary ballet is somewhere in the centre. Jooss varies from the centre to the second extreme. In his masterpiece, *The Green Table*, he has a powerful message to convey. The most powerful and moving moment of that message are the opening and closing scenes where the diplomats are gathered round the table. This is told with the very minimum of movement. Jooss is always at his very best with a social message to convey which he does, so to speak, in basic movement, so that nothing gets between the message and the audience. To my mind he fails when he is light or flippant because his work lacks variety and the ornamentation that is pleasing for its own sake. His *Company at the Manor* and Leeder's *Sailor's Fancy* are both works that call for an extended technique since their theme is trivial. Compare *Sailor's Fancy* with Massine's *Les Matelots* or Zulig's recent *Le Bosquet* and any of the versions of *The Gods Go a'begging* and my meaning will be obvious. The Jooss dancers, especially the men, are magnificently trained and follow the rhythm of the music as do few ballet dancers at the present day just because of this monotony of movement. Their facial expression tends to be stereotyped and they are very much the puppets of a remarkable producer. There can be no two opinions about Kurt Jooss's importance in the contemporary world of the dance and I must make it quite clear that what I am going to say is personal. Temperamentally I favour ballet that is nearer the extreme of dancing for the sake of dancing, because once the message of a *Green Table* has made its effect and I have admired the skill of the achievement I feel that there is little left.

Q. Is Jooss right in objecting to the use of the *points*?

A. In so far as he is thinking of his own ballets and his dramatic needs, possibly yes. In general, no ; he and most of us give this whole question too much importance. We must realise that the whole era of "toe-dancing" has gone. If ballet dancing is a complete system of physical education, then why quarrel at an extra inch. There is nothing brutal about the use of the toes. It comes perfectly natural to cossacks without the use of block shoes ; and the exaggerated block, a loathsome thing, is a recent American importation. If we can stamp out improper teaching, the hot-house forcing of young pupils to satisfy teachers' and parents' vanity, this whole discussion will die a natural death. That is one of the major aims of the Royal Academy of Dancing.

Q. You are very scathing about competitions. Do you realise that the majority of them are in aid of an admirable charity?

A. I am, and that is quite beside the point. There is no reason why a charity should be made to excuse the harm that is being done to an art. This whole pot-hunting attitude is a wrong one which teachers and parents should do their utmost to discourage ; the best of them do.

Q. Has speech any part in ballet? I am thinking of *Comus*.

A. Speech has no part in ballet and its use would upset the whole balance of the arts, entirely changing the medium. The convention of ballet is that emotion is expressed through movement. *Comus* remains an experimental exception justified, at any rate historically, since it is based on the old English art form of the masque. Helpmann happens to speak verse admirably. The average dancer is dumb—as far as the stage is concerned—and the complex movement of ballet would not allow him the necessary breath to speak. The theatre can use some of the movements of the dance for a certain non-realistic type of play as Michael St. Denis realised before the war with his magnificent *Theatre des Quinze* ; that is another matter.

Q. Has filmed ballet any future ?

A. There are two things that you can do with the camera in ballet ; have it in a fixed place and photograph your actual ballet. The result will be a filmed ballet, flat, dull and of use only as a record, in which case it might be valuable. Or you can use those dramatic effects that the film alone can give, a shifting view-point, the close-up and so on. In that case you will inevitably upset the existing relationship between music and the dance. Imagine the interruption to the flowing line, if suddenly in the middle of *Les Sylphides* you had a close-up of the ballerina. It would therefore be necessary to find an entirely new technique that took into account the nature both of ballet and the camera, to devise cine-choreography in fact. That is possible, but it seems to me that Walt Disney has already done so in a very remarkable manner, especially in those early Silly Symphonies and in the *Casse Noisette* sequence of *Fantasia.*

Q. Do you include tap or any other form of dancing in a dancer's education and can you call it complete without ?

A. I thought that question would come up sooner or later since so many teachers in your town advertise a complete dance education ; ballet, musical comedy, ballroom, acrobatic and tap. Ballet and ballroom are certainly in no way antagonistic but an early choice must be made between tap and ballet. Tap is very harmful to ballet. Incidentally how very, very few white people can tap at all. Bill Robinson, a negro, and indeed nearly all coloured dancers make a real art of tap dancing, relating it to some theme or mood. An Astaire, an exception in any case, does not depend on tap alone. He is a dancer of real brilliance. Is there anything more unpleasant than those horribly knowing youngsters who tap, tap, tap their way through competitions or whom one sees in the films aping their elders in songs and dances that they should not understand? It is high time parents understood the evils of such exhibitionism.

So-called acrobatic dancing very rarely contains any dancing at all, but if by that contortionism of any kind is implied, then it most certainly has no place in the ballet dancer's training. The sight of a woman being thrown about by two men is one of the most revolting spectacles one can see on the stage.

As for musical comedy dancing as practised in this country, I don't rightly know what that means unless it is ballet dancing robbed of its technique and well spiced with sex appeal. The truth is that managers here simply do not know how to use dancers in revue or musical comedy. I am thinking of the particular cases of two outstanding young dancers who have been doing such work for some time; they haven't yet been produced effectively and far less capable or well-trained persons could take their places at any moment. In America ballet dancers have been used in musical comedy with dazzling effect, and much as I regret seeing dancers of the quality of Toumanova, Baronova, Osato and others outside a ballet company, it does show that the producers know their job. A complete dance education includes ballet and the national dances of various countries; it often includes fencing, but this all-embracing curriculum invariably produces something very cheap and very nasty.

Q. Isn't that very narrow-minded? A lot of people enjoy these things, and after all a girl must earn a living since there is room in ballet for very few.

A. Then, according to you, because a lot of people enjoy the cinema organ or crooning a musical critic is narrow-minded when he condemns or ignores them as having nothing to do with music? That is a very dangerous argument. If I was concerned in these lectures with the way a girl earned her living I would have talked to you about typists and secretaries, nurses and shop assistants. We are not talking of economics or sociology but about an art in which for a number of reasons there is room for only a very few; that is a characteristic of all the arts.

Q. At what age should a child start training for ballet? Is fifteen too old?

A. That is a difficult question to which to give a positive answer because so much depends upon the physique and mentality of the individual. In Russia the Imperial Schools did not take a pupil until the age of ten and that gives you a rough guide. I don't mean that before that age the child should do no dancing. Pre-ballet dancing should be something free, not concerned with a rigid technique, something that develops the musical sense. I am convinced that to-day most of our children begin ballet proper far too young. The whole thing is rushed through at a pace that is bad for body and mind. Those great ballerinas of yesterday and the day before never knew what it was to have foot or leg trouble. Their bodies had been properly conditioned. As to the second part of your question, fifteen is, of course, on the old side for starting, but there could be exceptions; I have seen some.

Q. Does ballet dancing produce a strain on the heart?

A. Certainly not; dancers are exceptionally long lived. Here are a few rough figures from memory: Petipa 85, Johannsen 93, Cecchetti 82; the great ballerinas Preobrajenska, Egorova and Kchesinskaare all teaching very many hours a day and they are all well over 60. Dancers are not competing with anyone or with the stop-watch, but making harmonious movements for which they have been trained.

Q. How do you account for the enormous popularity of ballet? Is it escapism?

A. Escapism may play some part, but that is by no means the whole thing. What I call true escapism is when you live in a hovel and are so excited by the millionaire's palace you see on the film in your nearest Odeon, itself a palace, that you forget to complain about your hovel. Ballet, music and painting give what the Greeks call *re*-creation, the ability to gain strength from what you have seen so that you can face your problems better. I know of one very busy doctor who goes to the ballet at every opportunity. In his own words, "I see so much ill-health and lack of harmony that I go to the ballet to learn about perfect health and harmony."

Q. How can we in the provinces see more ballet? The demand is there; when the Wells visits us, which is very rarely, it is almost impossible to get seats.

A. I am always asked that question and I can give no satisfactory reply. You cannot mass-produce fine orchestras, theatrical or ballet companies. In ballet the problem is not so much that of dancers as of the choreographers to make them dance. One very partial solution that I strongly advocate would be a duplicate Wells company doing the same ballets, interchanging dancers at times, the one touring when the other company is in London.[1]

Question by Lecturer. But let me ask you a question in my turn. Have you got a municipal theatre?

Answer (from Listener). No.

Lecturer's Comment. You are, of course, lucky to have a theatre at all, even if it is wilfully misused. Many large cities—Gloucester is an example—have no theatre, so that even if there were enough ballet companies, they would have no stage. Your own theatre here gives the most dreadful rubbish, *Girls and Curls—a Musical Extravaganza, Laughs and Blushes—the Sex*

[1] This has now come about.

Appeal Show, and so on, week in and week out. The theatre may be full at the moment because the vast temporary war population must go somewhere to shelter from the rain, but these theatre managers are either ignorant or cynical in the extreme. They are bad citizens. And all the time you have the remedy in your hands. As ratepayers, demand an arts centre with a theatre and withhold a vote for any councillor who refuses it. If the rates go up as a result, it is well worth the extra money in the pleasure you receive and the good it will do your children, or, to put it negatively, the harm that it will prevent. Some councils seem to think it a real virtue to keep the rates low and some poor boobs are always taken in by the imagined economy. These present shows, pantomimes included, are quite unfit for your kids or for you, and for the first time you are in a very strong position. You have a new friend C.E.M.A. (now the Arts Council of Great Britain). C.E.M.A. is one of the fine constructive ventures the war has produced, the perfect solution to that problem of a Ministry of Fine Arts. It doesn't pauperise the theatre ; on the contrary it helps those who are trying to help themselves. Build your arts centre and then ask C.E.M.A. for music, opera, ballet or an art exhibition and you will get them, provided by a panel of experts that no theatrical concern could afford to assemble. The remedy is yours and don't be side-tracked, don't tolerate excuses. I am talking especially to the many schoolgirls in my audience. You learn all about civics. Get acquainted with C.E.M.A. and its workings. As soon as you get a vote, if your parents haven't already done the job, use it to give this city a worthy arts centre. The present state of affairs is an absolute disgrace not to be tolerated by anyone with an atom of civic pride.

Q. Why is ballet technique such an uncertain quantity? Whenever I see *Swan Lake* or any of the classics the dancers always seem to wobble and it worries me.

A. You have hit on something very important there. It is not a question of ballet technique but of the modern dancer. I can guarantee that neither Pavlova nor Genée ever wobbled, as you so expressively put it. The modern dancer is in a sense a utility dancer, she has been turned out too quickly without the poise and perfect sense of balance that long work at the *barre* alone can give. She is not sure of herself and doesn't always understand the aim of her work. Consequently she tries to fit in far too much, three imperfect turns instead of two perfect ones. That also becomes a musical fault. Pavlova, never a brilliant technician, at the end of her days when her technique was getting worn, was highly skilled in disguising this by attempting the very minimum that the music demanded. No ordinary audience noticed this and the result was no sacrifice of poise or balance. I am not saying that young dancers can or should make such drastic cuts, but that they will always get better results when they realise that interpretation and not virtuosity is the aim. Margot Fonteyn has long understood this.

Q. What about those thirty-two *fouettés* in *Swan Lake* ? They can't be cut.

A. Why not ? They always worry me exceedingly ; many of the great Russian ballerinas never attempted them and they tell us very little about a dancer. I know a number of children in Preobrajenska's studio who can turn fifty, sixty or seventy ; but no one would have called them dancers at that stage. Pavlova could never have attempted them. They should only be included when they are not a stunt, that is when the particular ballerina has the gift of performing them easily and correctly.

Q. My daughter who is learning ballet tells me that all the movements have French names. Isn't that making an unnecessary complication ?

A. Not at all ; the movements are in any case new and unfamiliar and are best described in a new vocabulary. The important thing is that ballet as an art is international and for historical reasons its language is French. Your daughter could join a Russian company to-morrow and be thoroughly at home with the work ; granted always that with her English-French could be understood the speakers of Russian-French !

Q. I am interested in this question of national aptitude for ballet through physique, temperament, etc. I know that you are a staunch champion of our national ballet ; in your frank opinion is the British dancer as talented as the Russian.

A. Speaking in terms of the *average* dancer there can still be no comparison. The young Russian dancer has a greater aptitude and there are a number of reasons for that. Ballet for a long time has been a traditional vocation. The Russians have superb teachers both in and out of the emigration, all of whom rose to fame on the stage as artistes of the dance. It is to three teachers that we owe that wonderful de Basil company of 1933 ; to Preobrajenska, a teacher of real genius, to Kchesinska and to Egorova. Their artistry was to be seen in every one of their pupils. Those girls were beautifully placed from the very start and had all the large movements so characteristic of the Russian school. That, of course, does not altogether answer your question because you talked of talent rather than opportunity. It is a little difficult to separate the two. Where the average Russian girl excels is in her whole attitude, in her will to excel. She is far more single-minded. She does not, for instance, allow marriage to interfere with her career.

But I am still a strong partisan of our ballet as distinct from our dancers. We have discipline, the lack of which has so damaged the *emigré* Russian Ballet, and under Ninette de Valois our ballet has an integrity that compares with that of Diaghileff. A Fonteyn and a Helpmann equal the finest of the Russians, and when I think of Beryl Grey, Moira Shearer, Margaret Dale or Pauline Clayden, to take some names at random, it is evident that we have real quality—and there are others. In the short history of our ballet that is quite extraordinary. I have watched the progress of our dancers in class and on the stage and its steady tempo gives me a very real confidence in their future. They have a certain inbred shyness to overcome, the national instinct that it is not quite good form to excel over their fellows. They still lack the attack so characteristic of the Russians. That is being eradicated bit by bit.

Q. Who is the best dancer you have ever seen ?

A. I once asked Fokine that question and was soundly rebuked. There is no best dancer, in an absolute sense ; there are best dancers for types of role. Let us stop grading dancers and do away with the competitive or fan atmosphere which is so very harmful to ballet. I am sickened by some of the unbalanced people who cluster round the stage door calling their favourites by their Christian names and praising them to the skies. They are a dreadful nuisance to the dancers they follow and a real danger to the young dancer who may possibly believe what they say. Not one of these " fans " has any real standards by which to judge ; to them Pavlova, Genée, Karsavina, Lopokova, Spessiva, Trefilova, are just names ; if they have heard of them at all. No, there is a small company of great dance artistes, but no best.

Q. Is there any practical method of dance notation ? Modern works are in danger of being lost.

A. There are various systems and in the case of the classics notation or even verbal description is possible. Not in the case of modern works. Think of a *Miracle in the Gorbals* with the whole cast acting or an *Adam Zero* with its complex movement to a complex score. I defy anyone to produce a workable system. That may be a very good thing. The classics alone are enduring, that is why they are classics. Ballets expressing the contemporary scene date within a decade or so. That was the opinion of Balanchine in a conversation I once had with him.

Q. I don't like ballet. I've tried hard. Is there anything I can do ? Is there anything wrong with me ?

A. Don't worry. I don't like carrots and I've tried very hard indeed. There is nothing wrong with you. There may even be something wrong with the ballet you've seen. I saw a company the other day . . . ! Ballet to be bearable must be very good indeed.

Q. How does one become a ballet critic ? This whole question of standards worries me.

A. It worries me too. The only thing that makes a critic is experience. Many people who have only made a recent acquaintance with ballet wish to be critics. The danger is the fact that they can have as yet no standards. They cannot measure what they see against Diaghileff and his brilliant company. Who can say what a perfect performance of *Swan Lake* should be without the memory of Trefilova, of *Giselle* without Pavlova or Spessiva, *Le Spectre de la Rose* without Karsavina, a performance of *Les Sylphides* not under the control of Fokine and so on ?

I have never, as my record shows, had the slightest sympathy with those who always invoke the past to condemn the future. They are invariably unmitigated bores. But the fact exists that the immediate past in ballet was an exceptionally glorious one that has set up standards for a very long time. The tempo of life to-day means that the education of the dancer has been speeded up at the sacrifice of perfection. The critic must have that perfection against which to measure every performance. I wonder where to-day's critics are to look ? A lowering of standards would bring very serious consequences. It is indeed a problem. The same problem exists for our dancers.